by John Yau

Poetry and Prose

Crossing Canal Street (1976)
The Reading of an Ever-Changing Tale (1977)
Sometimes (1979)
The Sleepless Night of Eugene Delacroix (1980)
Notarikon (1981)
    (with drawings by Jake Berthot)
Broken Off by the Music (1981)
Corpse and Mirror (1983)
Dragon's Blood (1989)
    (with artwork by Toni Grand)
Genghis Chan: Private Eye (1989)

Editor

The Collected Poems of Fairfield Porter (1985)
    (with David Kermani)

Criticism

BRICE MARDEN: A Vision of the Unsayable (1988)

JOHN YAU

RADIANT SILHOUETTE

NEW & SELECTED WORK
1974–1988

BLACK SPARROW PRESS
SANTA ROSA
1989

RADIANT SILHOUETTE: NEW & SELECTED WORK 1974–1988. Copyright © 1989 by John Yau.

All rights reserved. Printed in the United States of America. No part of this book may be used or reproduced in any manner whatsoever without written permission from the publisher except in the case of brief quotations embodied in critical articles and reviews. For information address Black Sparrow Press, 24 Tenth Street, Santa Rosa, CA 95401.

ACKNOWLEDGMENTS

The poems in this book are drawn from the following collections: *The Reading of an Ever-Changing Tale*, Nobodaddy Press, 1977; *Sometimes*, Sheep Meadow Press, 1979; *The Sleepless Night of Eugene Delacroix*, Release Press, 1980; *Broken Off by the Music*, Burning Deck, 1981; *Corpse and Mirror*, Holt, Rinehart and Winston, 1983 and *Dragon's Blood*, published by Gervais Jassaud and Collectif Generation, 1989. Some of these poems appeared in *Central Park, Hambone, Notus, o-blek, Parkett, Spazio Umano* (Milan), *Sulfur*, and the anthology *Broadway 2*. "A Cameo Of A Chinese Woman on Mulberry Street" was first published as a postcard by Bellevue Press. *Corpse and Mirror* was selected by John Ashbery to appear in the National Poetry Series. "Radiant Silhouette" was commissioned by Chris Bruce, Curator, and the Henry Art Gallery, University of Washington, Seattle, and first appeared in the catalogue *Cities*, which accompanied a three person exhibition: photographs by Marsha Burns; photographs by Michael Burns; pastels by Randy Hayes. "Eskimo Villanelle" was commissioned by Jim Rose for an exhibition of drawings by John Lees at Compass/Rose (Chicago). The revisions I have made are, for the most part, slight and concerned with clarity.

 A grant from the New York Foundation for the Arts (1988) helped greatly during the writing and editing of part of this book.

J. Y.

This project is funded in part by the California Arts Council, a state agency. Any findings, opinions, or conclusions contained therein are not necessarily those of the California Arts Council.

 Black Sparrow Press books are printed on acid-free paper.

LIBRARY OF CONGRESS CATALOGING-IN-PUBLICATION DATA

Yau, John, 1950-
  Radiant silhouette : new & selected work, 1974-1988 / John Yau.
    p.   cm.
  ISBN 0-87685-773-X. — ISBN 0-87685-774-8 (signed). — ISBN 0-87685-772-1 (pbk.)
  I. Title.
PS3575.A9R34   1989
811'.54—dc20   89-17498
                                                                               CIP

For Jane Hammond

Table of Contents

1974–1979

Cameo of a Chinese Woman on Mulberry Street	15
Their Shadows	16
After Moving	17
Ten Songs	18
"E Pluribus Unum"	19
The Reading of an Ever-Changing Tale	20
Shimmering Pediment	21
January 18, 1979	22
Robert Herrick	23
Chinese Villanelle	24
Marco Polo	25
Nantucket	26
Flying Inland	28
The Return of the Hunters	29
If You Asked	31
Serenade	32
Sometimes	34
Dear . . .	35

THE SLEEPLESS NIGHT OF EUGENE DELACROIX (1980)

Postcards from Nebraska	41
Predella	46
A Different Prince	48
The Discovery of Honey	54
The Clay Nursing Home	58
The Sleepless Night of Eugene Delacroix	61

The Noise of Life	63
Toy Trucks and Fried Rice	68
Electric Drills	72
The Telephone Call	75

BROKEN OFF BY THE MUSIC (1981)

Scenes from the Life of Boullee	81
Late Night Movies I	97
Late Night Movies II	99
Late Night Movies III	101
Late Night Movies IV	104
Shanghai Shenanigans	106
Rumors	107
The Dream Life of a Coffin Factory in Lynn, Massachusetts	109
Avenue of Americans	111
A Different Cereal	113
Broken Off by the Music	115

CORPSE AND MIRROR (1983)

Two Kinds of Song	121
Missing Pages	122
The Pleasures of Exile	124
Corpse and Mirror I	126
Corpse and Mirror II	130
Corpse and Mirror III	133
Variations on Corpse and Mirror	135
Variations on Corpse and Mirror (Second Set)	139
Two Meditations on Guanajuato	140
Carp and Goldfish	145

CHILDHOOD (1984)

Cenotaph	151
Cenotaph of Snow	154

Halfway to China	156
We Are All Vultures	160

DRAGON'S BLOOD (1985–1988)

Cascade	163
Seance Music	165
All This Changing Trouble Luck and Suddenness	166
Confessions	167
Paradise	168
Recoil	169
The Charred Voice of Max Ernst	170
You Must Remember	171
Red Fountain	173
Medusa	174
Return of Ulysses I	176
Return of Ulysses II	177
Why Did What Was When	178
Engines of Gloom and Affection	179
Dream Report	180
Dragon's Blood I	181
Dragon's Blood II	182
Dragon's Blood III	183
Dragon's Blood IV	184
Choral Amphisbaena	185
No One Ever Tried to Kiss Anna May Wong	187
Sam Spade Haiku	188
Genghis Chan: Private Eye I	189
Genghis Chan: Private Eye II	190
Genghis Chan: Private Eye III	191
Genghis Chan: Private Eye IV	192
Genghis Chan: Private Eye V	193
Genghis Chan: Private Eye VI	194
Genghis Chan: Private Eye VII	195
Texas Sprawl	196
La Brea	197
Manhattan Miniature	199

Spin, Spell, Spill	200
Picture Book	202
Predella	203
A Suite of Imitations Written After Reading Translations of Poems by Li He and Li Shang-yin	210
Eskimo Villanelle	212
Eskimo Tales	213
Radiant Silhouette I	214
Radiant Silhouette II	216
Radiant Silhouette III	218
Radiant Silhouette IV	220
Radiant Silhouette V	222
Bare Sheets I	224
Bare Sheets II	225
Bare Sheets III	226
Modern Love	227

Radiant Silhouette:

New & Selected Work

1974–1988

1974–1979

Cameo of a Chinese Woman on Mulberry Street

Her face this moon a house
always nearing the end of its road

from within each room
rising rising

slowly up through their sleep
for a breath

the pale fur and dark wings
the silver beak and silver talons

Their Shadows

According to my mother,
unlike most English farmer's daughters,
my grandmother had social pretensions.
Yet this opinion does not explain why
she decided to marry my grandfather.
In 1916, he taught, while the rest of England
fought in the muddy trenches of World War I.
"I do not think many Chinese fought in that war"
was my father's only remark.

If anything, this is their achievement
and their fame. He died in Hong Kong
shortly before she died in Liverpool.
My father was informed by two letters;
one from an aunt, one from a solicitor.
Nothing left to him in either case,
but their shadows mingling on his face.

After Moving

Even as the street becomes familiar to you
        almost incidental
the way details in novels can add
        their unblendable color
to the overall scheme; and faces pass
        from strangers to companions
without the intervention of touch;
        and the traffic
no longer sounds harsh, but grows muted
        as the gray afternoons
that occasionally fill the sky with a festering sun
        behind clouds rubbed smooth;
you feel removed from the surrounding scenery
        though if you were asked
you would not deny you have a place
        in this circumstance
and partake of events, though they rarely
        if ever
seem connected as the streets do
        angles of one block
joined to another, the buildings jammed together,
        with a child playing on the stoop
or covering her eyes while her friends
        run into the darkness
the game takes into account

Ten Songs

Trying to find a way to say something that would make it
    make its sense
Trying to find a way to weigh something that would make
    its own lens
Finding it trying to say something they would make
    a lens of
Finding the saying of something
weighing the sense of it trying

Making the trying something that would find its sense
Sensing the making trying to find something it says
Saying the finding is there to find is making it make sense
Making it make sense is finding something to say
Something to say is finding a lens to sense the making
Something making the making something something else

"E Pluribus Unum"

It is no longer necessary for sunlight
to reach here; this kitchen with its
linoleum floor; its scuffed roses

The light has been here all along
waiting for you to reach toward it
like a fish tinged by the ocean

The Reading of an Ever-Changing Tale

Certain colors got lodged under
the fingernails before their names
came to grace our speech.
                                  But
what of the phenomena whose
colors can only be imagined?
What did you do with the pills?
And why were you without any gasoline?
Today, these questions are a restraint
on your memory as the color
"blue" is a box opened up
like a sky under which
no grass grows. But traces remain.
The war you only just heard about
inextricably mixed with a face
you will probably never see again.

Shimmering Pediment

An overloaded circuit — lightning
Jammed the horizon, and for days
The echoes remained in my eyes.
But the brightest star is to begin
Anywhere. "Among the peonies,"
As an ancient Chinese poet wrote . . .

Near where the river pirouettes
Past the airplane graveyard
I wandered in as a child;
A fenced-in-field; the broken
Fuselages and crumpled wings
Reclining, like sunbathers, in
Haphazard rows of damaged magnificence.

Actually, I never played on this knoll,
Though I think somehow I must have.
For around supper I felt compelled
To return to that silent and empty
Amphitheater, my plane spiraling
In a diminishing circle, as I flew
Parallel to where I am now standing.

January 18, 1979

So often artists have painted a woman
washing or combing her hair.
And nearby is a mirror.
And there you were,
crouched in the tub.
It was cold in the apartment.
It is always cold in winter.
But you were brushing out your hair
and singing to yourself.
And, for a moment, I think
I saw what those artists saw—
someone half in love with herself
and half in love with the world.

Robert Herrick

I like wallpaper that makes sense.

I own and operate a gas station
that stands neatly clustered on a wedge
formed by a fork in the road.
The dust is a hindrance, but not a veil

Even on overcast days I can see my face,
like the shell of a scooped-out cantaloupe,
rising in the windshields.
And, sometimes, at night, I can see its ellipse
floating toward me, as if
what it was going to say this time
would make today a departure
from all the rest.

In the afternoon the lake is as smooth
as the polished black hood
of Mr. Meriwether's vintage '38 Cadillac.
It has that bottomless dark feeling about it
that only cars and lakes and you can have.

Chinese Villanelle

I have been with you, and I have thought of you
Once the air was dry and drenched with light
I was like a lute filling the room with description

We watched glum clouds reject their shape
We dawdled near a fountain, and listened
I have been with you, and I have thought of you

Like a river worthy of its gown
And like a mountain worthy of its insolence . . .
Why am I like a lute left with only description

How does one cut an axe handle with an axe
What shall I do to tell you all my thoughts
When I have been with you, and thought of you

A pelican sits on a dam, while a duck
Folds its wings again; the song does not melt
I remember you looking at me without description

Perhaps a king's business is never finished,
Though "perhaps" implies a different beginning
I have been with you, and I have thought of you
Now I am a lute filled with this wandering description

Marco Polo

Recently he has turned to us and said: "It's bizarre to think about the brain firing and then not firing." Yet this new remark of his does not clarify why the two episodes he has told us about are separated by a park in the shape of a brain. He claims he does not understand how windows can exist apart from their settings; or that buildings (this hospital, for example) are only incidental to the narrative unfolding around them. It is necessary that I persuade him of the possibility. For aside from what could be brought back as cargo, he carried everything else in his mind. Perhaps we should (as one of us has suggested) move him to another room; one whose windows face the mountains, or perhaps the bay where we first stood and watched in disbelief.

Nantucket

It was late in the afternoon when I returned with the paper bag. I had been cradling it in the crook of my right arm, and steadying it with my left hand, as if the bag contained a plant of some sort. Sweat darkened my shirt and made my forehead glisten, like a car fender in the rain, by the time I slid sideways into the cottage by nudging the screen door with my shoulder. Something either I or the cat started doing last summer

I realized how light the bag was, only after I placed it on the kitchen table, and began looking for the scissors. It's an ordinary paper bag with a dark brown stain on one side. Perhaps it once contained some apples, one of which was rotten, or a damp pair of gardener's gloves and a screwdriver. As I knelt beside the only road on this end of the island, a long bright car sped by, and someone's hand let the bag flutter down beside me, as if they knew what I needed then.

How else could I have carried the skeleton home? It was lying on its side beneath a row of raspberry bushes, and looked—because of the seaworthy curve of its bones—like a half-finished model of a whaling ship.

Usually such a model is placed inside a bottle. I suppose, yes, it is a testament to the craftsmen to be amazed by the number of details they managed to include. Cannon, captain's table, lamp and winch: these things should not be taken for granted, though I feel that what anyone really wants to find when they look into a bottle is that an essential element has been overlooked. A marred perfection is what the viewers (and I must, for a moment, align myself with them) are after, though not of the kind those craftsmen attained.

It was once a puppy, that much is obvious. There is a white plastic collar around its neck, and not one of the rhinestones is missing. It was the collar that made me want to take it home. It underlined the weight of the bones in a way that nothing else could. I knew immediately that this skeleton (bones and jewelry) was the perfect memento of this island, this scrap of grass and rock that used to wait for the whaling ships to return, their holds full of oil. And in the pocket of each sailor some scrimshaw.

Flying Inland

The pilot looked out of the cockpit window and (as the city vanished beneath the monaural clouds) began thinking of how, except for a few isolated specifics, a face tends to become a blur. The chipped tooth. The two small scimitar scars emblazoned on the chin after lurching off the porch. The mole on the right shoulder blade. The color of her hair on a rainy March Thursday as the birthday cake slipped from his hands.

Unlike Ulysses, it is unclear what happened to the Trojan Horse. Perhaps because there was nothing to return to. The muddy lake bottom causes the head to tilt, like a dog does when it's looking at its master, perplexed by his most recent command. From the road that was stuck in like a word between the mountains and the water, the shepherd (or is it Ulysses) stares back at it.

After many hours of tugging and pulling, the villagers manage to pull the hollow, waterlogged body ashore. The clapping and singing could be heard for miles, carried from tree to tree. A young woman dances in her bare feet, the mud oozing sweetly between her toes, while in the background the shepherd is sitting and drinking beer. He is wondering what he has found, and what he has already started to overlook.

The Return of the Hunters

Anywhere is conterminous with another,
the glossy touched-up photographs
illustrating months in a calendar
from a mutual life insurance company.
August is a pink carnivorous plant.
March and September are green
and red reptiles, the former
a frog carved from soft dark stone;
its wide peering face,
like a useful grin out of Othello,
almost fills the allotted space.
And pressed close to the sides of
its mouth are the front feet
terminating in incised claws
(an indication this represents
not a true frog, but a saurian monster).
The carefully polished stone
recreates the effect of wet
or slimy amphibian skin.
May is a yellow marble statue of a boy
sunk up to his chest in torrential mud.
January is an abandoned blue monastery.
The wind is lifting the loosely packed snow
into a dance of the seven veils without dancers.
This month is a pleasure cruise,
a brown and gray ferry that shuttles
berry stained vacationers
among the Thousand and One islands.
The crowded deck lists slightly.

And there is a grasping stillness
in all of the festivities; in
leaving the pier; as if somehow,
in moving, everything would be
shattered and undone.
You are arched over the railing,
one in a line of families, lovers,
Australian businessmen,
estranged uncles, and nuns.
The engines have started to churn
their welcome turmoil up
onto the lake's flat expanse.

If You Asked

No it didn't get too cold here too often.
Expectations flare around the morning
sliding down its sluice,
and are swallowed later,
like an aspirin.
The clouds unfurl elsewhere.
The hope of an answer is held out as an answer.
A helmet of haze settles,
and doorways are remembered by the rain
that brought us there, and released us
later from its shimmering cage.
Shadows have toppled across roofs
and down brick in blue planks,
while pigeons rise from our feet.
I too glisten, and, like a tray of silverware
appearing suddenly within the circle
of the burglar's flashlight,
I look for what I have overlooked.
Was it only the seamstresses blushing
in colors no one dreams of anymore?
And what is there to say now,
without going on
like the threads
of a frayed scarf?

Serenade

The windows reflect the fuscous clouds.
Why are we always wondering about
what is going on offstage?
At first, we called these glimpses dreams,
but that moonlit jail was soon overcrowded.
And sometimes it was a lot.
So, we began changing the headlines,
and what we could not understand
(like a lunchbag left in the rain)
became a talk that was no talk,
a talk that was almost incoherent,
except that each of us understood perfectly.
"Another language," we said, "not merely
an economy of words so spare
that one word is made to do the work of hundreds."

The torn postcard lay beside a pile of sawdust.
There are three people (more likely
there are five) sitting in the dining car
of the unnamed train
(The Sunset Fuselage Express,
The Fortunate Fossil,
and others hurtle through the mist).
Outside, the dazzling yet almost familiar trees
melt into an even more familiar mahogany corridor.

"Yes, I have decided to introduce you to everyone.
The woman on the far right is Celeste,
and next to her is Aunt Gladys and Uncle Hank,

Mighty Morrisey and Yellow Duck Fever.
Then, there is the rather well dressed man
about whom I can tell you nothing
you don't already know.
Do not look puzzled.
Such things are bound to happen, and
certainly you have grown accustomed
to the possibility."

The leather glove is draped over the silver cane;
its handle has been hammered
into the head of Medusa, and its eyes
are inlaid with diamond chips;
bright concavities; bright as a sea in which
an island rises; a place that remembers
anyone approaching it.

Sometimes

What I think I am looking for is a place
to hang my hat and park my shoes.
But, for the moment, not even that is necessary.
I distrust smiles that precede their owners,
even if there is only one cafe and this table
and this chair on this island.
For most of the evening I have sat here
undisturbed, watching the island
moored to the rusted schooner and vice versa.

The numbers on the wooden seats —
almost like an old creaking stadium —
are now only a reminder of when
there were people who needed to find them
on the way back from the bar, the bathroom, or both.
The stars are like that too, fading chairs,
their numbers painted on in a language
where numbers are unimportant.

Dear . . .

    I know you hardly ever leave your room now
            and perhaps
this letter will remain in the mailbox
            for months
only to stare out through the grating,
            white in that
shallow black space, like the moon
            in the mirror
of a one room basement apartment
on a seedy waterfront street,
            its smooth face
like an Indian Head nickel is
            partially blocked
by four cast iron bars (recently painted red)
            installed against thieves
            and other unwanted guests.

It is a clear night, for the moon
            has traveled
below street level the way commuters do
            half a block away
though it is a dirty "forgotten" station
            and the smell
is almost overpowering to the men and women
            familiar
with the steepness of its twenty-two steps
as they return to their rooms
            from the evening shift
at the doll factory near the unfinished highway.

On the other side of the street
(about ten yards before the basement window)
stand three aproned women.
        They are friends, and,
as in most cases, it is by circumstance.
        However,
this has not diminished their feelings of joy,
        which is the only word
that one of them uses to describe her recent engagement.
        For the moment
she will continue to live with her older sister
        in the house
closest to the river.

Across the street
two men walk separately,
as only one is employed by the doll factory.
        The other man,
Stefan, is an ambitious young bookbinder.
        He is carrying
a package delivered to him earlier today
        by courier
along with special constructions.
        The streetlight
illuminates a face deep in thought.
Stefan has only to remember the book.

On the plaque in the railroad station
that usually gives the name of the station
        are the words:
Behold the Dream of Frogs.
        Outside,
on the platform, a bruised young woman
        (O Psyche!, he thinks)
in a torn chiffon dress with a high collar
        holds a parasol.
A lock of her hair has slipped out from under her hat

and drifted down over her forehead
> while one tear

hangs precariously from her right eye
> like a jewel.

Behind the station are the twelve houses
comprising this nameless little town.
> Built

out of seashells shaped like Japanese fans,
their arrangement reflects an intense concern
> with symmetry.
> But

what he remembers most are the turtle shells
lining the streets instead of cobblestones;
> on each shell

is carefully engraved a frog, and in its left eye
> is a musician:

A squat mustachioed man with pointy ears
> tunes a violin;

a heavy jowled man with tiny feet squeezes his accordion
> and smacks his lips;

a thin tubercular woman with snarling lips
> taps her zither;

a churlish figure tries tying two harps together.
At least twenty-five hundred musicians are assembled,
> and each

is playing an instrument of one kind or another.
> Some are as familiar

as the trombone, while others are as unfamiliar
> as the oud.

Yet Stefan, who is feverish with understanding,
> knows

he is a witness to the most beautiful song in creation.
> A song

that will change him down to the colors
> he prefers.

After many hours of tedious gluing,

        he finds
he is almost home. Inside the books are the musicians
        as in his mind
their possibilities blaze like a fire
to which nothing (and nothing else)
        can be added.

The Sleepless Night of Eugene Delacroix
(1980)

Postcards from Nebraska

1

How do I get onto these trivial subjects? Only you are subject to them. Everyone else gets the major points in my life. You get the obscure subdivisions of subdivisions of minor points derived from other minor points which result from the major points everyone else knows about.

2

Today's earning came from babysitting for a seven year old girl who preferred to be called "Apple Crumb." I was interrupted early in the afternoon by her, and told to play one game of checkers (lost naturally!) and one game of Mastermind (also lost), though in this instance she knew more about the game, and won easily, without cheating or changing the rules, as far as I can tell.

3

Letter from X: trauma, resigned from job result of conflict with short slimy boss; sudden weight loss, gray hair, tears, worry, bladder infection, all consequence of the situation. New job: same type of position, better atmosphere, though no mention of relief.

4

The metronome of indecision continues its undercurrent of distraction. The feeling reminds me of certain parts of Virginia, a flat country broken up by trees.

5

My astrologer says: "Not a stone rolls in heaven but ripples in your pool." I want to ask her if I'm in serious trouble, but how can I at a time like this? I guess I have to discover those "non-grasping vantages" she has mentioned.

6

I'm back to back. And my big news at noon is that it is −12 outside, with a wind chill factor of −73. Needless to say, there is no chance I'm going outside (well, I did stand outside for a moment to feel what −73 felt like. And I'd say it felt like *death*). In fact there are advisors out alerting people that frostbite occurs very quickly and without warning during this kind of weather. According to these experts the only warning is numbness—but hell, Nebraska always leaves me numb.

7

Like the snow, the constant drone of the air conditioner in the summer is also a factor, along with the predominance of jeeps and marshmallow bread. There is a sense of the 1930s, late '20s, in many of the buildings. The two story motel with small windows, the pastel green and blue store fronts and garage doors. The screened-in hamburger and hot dog (in-the-round) stands. The dark green booths I sit in when I eat lunch. Yesterday, I heard the man behind me say: "My wife and I first visited a nudist colony in 1932, and we've been visiting organized nudist colonies ever since."

8

Even after all these years I feel like I'm learning so much new neat stuff: (e.g.: the most common cause of poisoning among young children is due to a sudden increase in salt. Little kids will grab the salt shaker off the table and consume all the salt in it. As it hits the stomach, it alters the osmotic pressure and the blood plasma rushes into the stomach, drastically shrinking the volume of blood circulating in the body—thus the electrolyte balance (ions and garbage) is way off; a real nasty nasty).

9

We spend a lot of time on obesity, which I find fascinating. We exploded the myth of the "middle age spread" and learned if a person overeats by 20 cal a day (1% of a 2000 cal intake, which is average for many) he or she will gain 2 lbs at the end of the year. Over 30 years that gain will amount to 60 lbs. This weight gain shows up in middle age, hence the myth.

10

One interesting highlight to all this is that I learned how to avoid sending your parents to an old age home. Actually it's a common occurrence out here. What happens is that the children take their senile parents on a vacation. This usually means somewhere far from home. Along the way they eliminate all forms of identification; labels and tags from dresses suits and gloves etc. Then they stop for lunch at a Howard Johnson's. When the parent or parents go off to the bathroom, the children drive off. It's quite difficult to trace where these people came from. And often they themselves don't know.

11

I'm having a good time these cloud-infested days though I'm not sure why. And can't tell if it's that bit of cake they give you before leading you to the guillotine.

12

Let me tell you, train rides are no different than boat rides. After half an hour all exuberance is gone.

13

The other class I'm taking is my biggie in terms of nerves diarrhea heart palpitations and tired feet. It is known as 497 by everyone who has it or will take it. It is justifiably famous. Much sympathizing goes on among those taking it and between the current takers and the former ones. The big line is: YEAH, but wait until you're kitchen manager.

14

If my letter seems weighty—you can always put a muzzle on me and send me out to bark at the policeman.

15

We have to serve the food from the left, the beverage from the right, always but always using the hand farthest away from the guest; never but never place ugly dirty thumb over the rim of the plate; remember to place the coffee cup and saucer within ½ inch of the edge of the table and please don't forget to place the butter at the 6 o'clock position on the bread and butter plate. Dear Sweet Morton Pilgrim Jr. (sounds like a Kurt Vonnegut name from his middle period) stands in the dining room grading us. I am always getting little yellow slips saying: did not place handle of coffee cup in 3 o'clock position.

16

I bought a ton of sesame seeds (at a reduced rate of course) for my roll making course and I hammered home the supports for my new shades which were bought in an attempt to spruce up my apt. (awful private tree).

17

Did I tell you I met him at an Edgar Cayce meeting? He always asks in-depth spiritual questions I can never answer.

18

I was in the middle of a fantasy and a pretty good one (pant pant), but I decided to forget it for you and a letter.

19

I'm saving more, but enjoying it less.
I'm saving it more, but enjoying less.
I'm enjoying it more, but saving less.
I'm enjoying more, but saving it less.

20

At any rate, one mild Sunday evening I came home to find an envelope taped to my screen door. It was an invitation to go to Deadly Dudley's the following Tuesday. The man's phone number and name were included. I assumed that the invitation was another case of mistaken identity. Being a good person I trotted across the street to the phone booth to call the man to tell him I was not who he believed I was. I got his answering service (sweet voice, no body) discovering in the process that he was a veterinarian. A few days later, I tried again, got him, and explained that this was "a case of mistaken identity." I protested for about four minutes, in the drugstore phone booth, told him that since I didn't know him he couldn't know me, etc. He then asked if I weren't the woman who spent spring semester running every morning in mauve gym shorts. I couldn't deny that now, could I?

21

I'm keeping my trip to Calgary for another time because it takes so long to treat the subject properly.

Predella

A blue woolen glove folded over like an old one dollar bill someone keeps hidden in their wallet, a crumpled galosh, a rubber boot half-submerged in slush (remnants of a scene of mismanaged violence).

A convoy of hats disperses into the evening. The night was pulling its shade over the city's dirty windows. Half a face pushes out of the darkness, a boxing glove, and veers off down the narrowing corridor. An intersection of voices—how not to be snagged there, like nylons catching on a calloused heel; a tear in the veneer. She thought about how she wiggled into her bra the way she settled into a role. By moving around until she was comfortable. On the radio a song celebrated the joys of love in sincerest doggerel.

Mounds of snow, complete with plateaus, threatening boulders, cliff faces, and the danger of avalanches.

Gray sky, gray underwear; everything was taking on the color of the city. As he bent down to pick his crumpled dungarees up from the floor, he was reminded of Claude Rains in *The Invisible Man*; the insane laughter echoing on the train platform; he had heard it again; the hatchet-faced man next to him in the diner reading the newspaper (he was, for some reason, wearing tan driving gloves); the story of a woman who killed and fed the family dog to her whining daughter and alcoholic husband. The headline was in bold type:

    MOM SERVES PUP STEW
    TO STEWED POP

Furrows of snow; perfectly preserved tire tracks. It was as if a city had started growing in a farmer's field, where he had, just the morning before, been plowing. Everyone teetered; some fell; a new kind of gravity; life on the moon.

Mrs. Garland was as thin and pale as the handkerchief she often twisted between her hands, while talking, continuing the story she had been telling for more than fifty years, or ever since her husband did not return one evening. Her best friend, Mrs. Central, was also thin, though in her case it was more a matter of bones than flesh. Her skin did not have, like her friend's, that quality of moonlight shining through paper windows, an image Mrs. Central often used to explain her humble origins, because, as she noted, "Since the Japanese live in paper houses, they must be extremely poor, though certainly neat and well mannered as everyone knows."

So much so the days would have to begin elsewhere.

A Different Prince

1

One name becomes two—Siegfried and Sassoon (or stop and shop as they sometimes murmured to each other while making love)—as a van door slides shut, and a woman's voice dissolves between the stars' hush and crickets' hum.

2

Piss trickled down the grassy incline.

3

Chopin, Falla, Sibelius.
The swan of Finland.
The swans of Manhattan.

4

The steady glow of the radio was diminished by the rhythmic pulsing of his cigarette. He was hunched over the steering wheel, staring into the long Kansas night. An occasional grain elevator lurched up out of the darkness. At the end of this tunnel was Aunt Sarah, who was anxiously waiting for the bad news, as she did every day. To Siegfried, the landscape was flat and relentlessly uneventful. Thousands of dinosaurs yearned here and died here. Thousands more soon will. He smiled cautiously at this last thought, his lips breaking into a parched, halting half-grin. He rolled the window down, flicked the cigarette out, and drove on, while Sassoon slept, curled on the mattress that took up most of the back of the van. Dreams flickered across her eyelids.

5

They both wanted to go to New York, ostensibly to see if they wanted to live there, which they did, though neither of them knew why or could advance a solid reason for going there. I haven't seen Aunt Sarah in nearly three years, Siegfried remarked one morning. Sassoon, who was about to sit down on the toilet, looked up and smiled. Siegfried smiled too.

6

In the haze of waxen sunlight Rupert shuddered small twitching sobs, as Siegfried and Sassoon waved goodbye and drove off. Determined not to be left behind, he crumpled Sunday's list of things to do, and stormed back into the small blue and orange cottage he rented from the silver haired philosopher. He began immediately and methodically tearing up all the magazines and books. The cat fled. Finally, exhausted by all that he had done, Rupert curled up beside a pile of torn pages and cried himself to sleep. When he woke up, he knew what he had to do next.

7

April, May, and June Wong sat primly in the back of their father's new black Dodge Dart, licking their pale green ice cream cones, and watching the man and woman emerge from their van and head for the bathrooms. I think he's kind of cute, April whispered to her nodding, sighing sisters.

8

Plato Wong stood halfway out of the phone booth, watching the man and woman slowly walking from the rest room area to the long chrome diner. A red neon YES flashed off and on. The woman stopped, stood on her toes and stretched out her arms, turned like a dancer. She undid her hair, letting lazy brown curls swirl down her back. The man walked on ahead.

9

I think the fumes are seeping further inland. I think our time is nearly up. Now we must decide what our action will be. And if there is none—only groomed humiliation—we must push forward anyway. Our faces gushing with the smiles of ones who know the outcome is inevitable. The destiny already decided. He held the phone gingerly, as if it were about to explode. He did this with everything, even his children.

10

As Plato walked to his car he passed the man and woman. The man was taller than Plato had at first thought. He was carrying a cardboard tray with two containers and two sandwiches wrapped in wax paper. The ends were twisted. The dark crevice of her opened red blouse snared his attention. Her smile flashed. It had claws.

11

Sarah married Bertrand in the hope that they would raise a large family of important children. Neither of them, as their own parents reminded them, would become more than what their grandparents were, little puddles of piss.

12

Sarah sat by the pink Princess phone remembering how the years slithered by without bringing them any children. She leaned her head against the wall and began crying once more, her massive body heaving with anxiety, frustration, and anger. The matted print of the white street by Maurice Utrillo seemed to be making a mockery of her feelings.

13

Bertrand stood in the kitchen, read the instructions, and then began carefully stirring the tomato bisque soup. Cooking has become humiliating he thought.

14

Plato watched the wind tugging at the pink kleenex. Waiting to be used, half out of its box, fluttering like a bird with one wing. The damp coolness of driving at night, the side vents open, was something Plato savored. The stars sinking down to join the horizon. Tail lights disappearing up ahead. Occasionally he would pass a truck or another car, his headlights illuminating a man deep in thought. Sometimes, the man would turn and look at him without any expression.

15

Sassoon drove through the piss of Missouri sunlight. So far they had avoided most of the turnpikes and had undulated along the secondary routes. Colorado seemed years away. She grew happier the further it receded into the pile of names she would never use again.

16

Like orgasm, she thought, a vast blank space evaporating beneath the stars. That's where I want to live. She wondered if Siegfried felt, could feel, the same way.

17

Suddenly, Sassoon felt depressed and turned on the radio. Siegfried continued sleeping, oblivious to Sassoon as she was to him. Sunlight filled the van and warmed the right side of his face. Another shadow limped beside the highway. A patch of breeze. She felt better.

18

Plato stopped and let the young man out. He drove off, leaving him to dwindle in the rear view mirror. In the back his daughters giggled and told each other dirty jokes they didn't quite understand.

19

Sarah wondered why she had done what she had done. Bertrand wondered why he hadn't. The gray light of the movie continued emptying into their apricot-colored bedroom.

20

A figure leaped out of the glare. Siegfried slammed on the brakes, and fishtailed to a stop. The man ran toward the van, while Siegfried put it in reverse. Sassoon mumbled something, and then closed her eyes again. She loved the coolness that lingered throughout the back of the van, and was glad she hung the bedspreads over the side windows. She loved the warmth her body made after it settled into the cool sheets. Sweat moistened her back, and a drop rolled slowly down her neck and between her breasts. She wondered why Siegfried had stopped when he had been in such a rush.

21

Hello Rupert.
Hello Siegfried, hello Sassoon.

22

They drove on silently.
By the way, what happened to our cat and plants?
I gave them to Brooke to care of. You know how she loves animals and things.
Yes, but she doesn't love us.

23

Rupert glanced at his watch, date and hour, as if he were late for an appointment, and then stared out the window. The plants were beginning to droop by now, the yellow creeping higher. The cat had never returned. Siegfried lit a cigarette. Sassoon was mad. She had wanted to leave everything behind, even friends.

24

Rupert wondered what Aunt Sarah was like. He hoped she would take care of him. As they approached the Holland Tunnel, the highway began filling with jostling cars. Siegfried wondered if there ever really would be too many cars and not enough highways. Soon they would be in New York. Soon he would be walking on unfamiliar streets. All around him angry drivers set their jaws in angry determination. The sun was setting. Sassoon slept, her breasts pointing in different directions, and, for the moment, she dreamed of no one in particular.

The Discovery of Honey

1

Through the fading years a town had fallen together on the side of the mountain that faced away from the sunset. A few stores remained open, though the streets were nearly empty. The new policeman turned left as he had done twenty-five minutes earlier. This time the speckled hand didn't rise above the yellowed curtains and wave.

2

It became clear to everyone, including her grandmother, when their Sunday dinners were infiltrated by innuendoes.

3

He wanted to tell her something he had never told any of his previous girlfriends, but every incident he remembered seemed mundane. Perhaps his only recourse was to invent a few details, a few moments of ardent activity in the dark corners of his New England hills. It went this way for a week or so. But nothing he thought of began with that tingling sharpness that characterized a quiet winter afternoon; an hour when the white clapboard houses settled deeper into the street, and the shadows shrugged off by the trees, the flagpole, and the soldier striding through the mall possessed sparkling violet tones among their varied contours.

4

It was Saturday, and everyone was lined up for the matinee. Above the sweaty throng was the newest billboard; a flower, a pair of glasses, a rainy day, a plastic shoehorn—according to the red and green words, these were the necessary ingredients.

5

"Sifting the colors of the rainbow is one activity that never quite lives up to its promise."
"Neither does brushing your teeth."

6

The collisions occurred all afternoon, and the after effects were noticeable to everyone. A man smoothing his bald head, a whimpering child, an eager woman staring in disgust.

7

The bed was lumpy, and the scratchy sheets clung to it, like burlap to potatoes. The coffee mugs were clean, but chipped. The hairbrush collected samples, while the toothpaste tube formed elfin green lumps. No one forgot about the bread crumbs.

8

Not only were the designs ingenious, but each clock emitted a unique sound. He was more of a doctor to them, a midwife; he knew the quirks residing in their bodies. However, today everything worked perfectly. The bishops, ants, and fish returned without knowing what they were supposed to do and did it.

9

"Sometimes, I think self-esteem is a parody of cities buried under tons of golden sand."
"Yes, and each fried egg is a reminder."

10

They were served breakfast by a young woman who had just graduated from high school; freckled, round, and tanned, like the pancakes; plump, awkward, and arrogant, like the sausages.

The owner was tall and gawky, a kind of featherless prehistoric bird. And when he was standing (which was about all he seemed capable of doing) he leaned forward every few seconds and stared into the mirror that took up a large part of the wall opposite him. He probably is a fixture in some seedy downtown bar, she thought, for he had a lopsided smile that looked as if it could snarl and smile in the same breath.

11

"This happiness is a rumor, our rumor, because no one believes it, yet everyone knows its birthday."

"If I am upset and say quicksand I am wrong. The weather would never allow such a thing to happen."

12

He was puttering in the kitchen, the red apron she bought him already covered with cake batter.

The radio station changed its program from Morton, Gottschalk, and Ives to "popular hit tunes" sung by groups who had not been the first to record them. Between the trumpets and the contralto she thought all these "about to be famous groups" should be called *The Footnotes,* but was too lazy to get up and change the station.

The cottage was a damp, faded cube whose interior had been refurbished by her mother's boyfriend, a retired mechanic, in various shades of brown and green, slashes of blue, symmetrical smears of red, and repetitions of yellow and white; they were reminders of summer, when the crackling winds drove powdery dunes across the lake; this hand mirror placed among the mountains, which were bound and gagged by the snow that came each winter, and only occasionally left in the spring as if it had never been there.

By the time the next music program came on, the clouds had hardened like bacon grease.

13

Alissa was the youngest child of the couple next door. He had heard about her before meeting her, and knew she was retarded, though he didn't realize until he met her that she was also a mongoloid.

"I wuv you," she would tell him. "You my boyfriend. And I am my own best girlfriend."

14

She stood and danced in the doorway of the other room so he couldn't see her, but he would know that he wasn't alone.

15

"The moon is already part of their wallpaper."

16

Her next pair of sunglasses wouldn't be as stupid as these, that's for sure.

17

Every time she pushed his tongue past her teeth, "like a mitten groping in the dark," she remembered how she used to roll cubes of jello around in her mouth when she was young. Apple, strawberry, watermelon, orange, lime, banana, root beer, and grape: she was running out of flavors and would soon have to tell him everything.

The Clay Nursing Home

At the Annual Clay Nursing Home White Elephant Sale and Picnic, Mrs. Charlotte Surge tittered coyly as she remarked to Mrs. Francine Powers: "There is nary a tarnished pachyderm to be spotted for miles, is there?" The innuendo was not lost on Francine, whose rotund, freckled young husband, Alfred, was busy, not ten yards away, dropping oranges in the nursing home's new juicemaker, his bald gleaming head (his "magnificent dome" as Francine liked to whisper) indifferent to everything but the sun. "In fact," Charlotte went on to say, "the abundance, the sheer abundance of interesting and worthwhile items, donated both freely and generously, proves the inherent goodness of everyone connected with the Clay Task Force."

(Long picnic tables formed right angles on the lawn, their white tablecloths lifting with each breeze.)

Francine agreed. She bared a proud white smile and pointed stiffly to the various objects she thought would bring a good price: twenty-four pairs of sneakers from THE SOFT SHOE; a note from Ulysses S. Grant informing a creditor, "You will just have to wait in line"; an ivory harmonica reportedly played by Ambrose Bierce when Pancho Villa ordered him shot; eight glass bricks from Mr. Child's FLOWER POWER (it had burned down in a mysterious fire on the previous Sunday; at least two dozen majolica pots; a matching pair of ceramic basket-carrying elephants (coveted by all) that had graced Mr. Child's front window for twenty-two years, and were known throughout the town (particularly its bars) as "Wetty" and "Crunch" (mayor and his wife's nicknames); Dr. Adamson's hand carved meerschaum pipe (Napoleon's tricolored hat) mounted on a wooden stand (carved by the bereaved Mrs. Adamson in her last years), and placed inside a glass case donated by the BARON'S TROPHY COMPANY; a hundred hand-painted postcards, each depicting a sight in and around Singapore (Raffles Hotel, etc.); a wagon wheel, slightly worm eaten, supposedly from a Conestoga wagon; a set of custom woks ("pretty stupid flower pots if you ask me," Mr. Child mumbled to no one in particular) from Mr. Kwo.

However, one of the items that was overlooked by Mrs. Surge and Mrs. Powers was a thin, waterlogged, leather bound octavo. Unknown to either them, or the present owners, it was a notebook Mallarmé bought in November 1866, shortly after he and his family moved to Besançon, so that he could teach at a lycée. The present owners were Mr. and Mrs. Lidstone. He was a custom furniture maker, who supplemented his income by teaching woodworking at the local high school. Everyone was hoping he would donate one of his custom made desks or chairs. Instead, the Lidstones brought the contents of their attic (adding to the already large array of birdhouses, cages, and feeders), and a full service for twenty-four. It might appear that such a set would be a highly desirable purchase, but the motif, two possums nuzzling each other "in a rather intimate way," was not what one expected to find "beneath the gravy," as Mr. Lidstone was known to mutter after Sunday dinner. In fact, it was on the previous Sunday, "the day of the fire," that Simon (as his wife called him) suddenly burst out with "sure do look like two skunks fucking, don't it?" to Father Williams, who tried his best to nod politely. It was after this dinner that Selma (as her husband sometimes called her) said, "It's either me or those damned dishes." Mr. Lidstone did not take this opportunity to do what he had been wanting to do for twenty years.

The notebook: neither Simon nor Selma could remember how it came into their possession, though he thought she must have bought it while they were traveling in France three summers ago, hoping to keep a record of their expenses. Only *his* wife would not have checked to see if the pages were clean.

She remembered that he had brought it home from France, after he was discharged from the Army in the spring of 1948. She wondered why, of all the things to bring back, he brought home a fading notebook full of sentences in a foreign language. What really got her miffed was that her husband did not understand one word of French, not that it mattered in this case. What was he doing over there for all those years anyway?

What was left was illegible, except for some letters from the author's name and the date the notebook was probably started. Otherwise, a lot of blue lines and ink ran together.

The Sleepless Night of Eugene Delacroix

In North Africa, Delacroix had seen a Jewish wedding which he described extensively in his journal:

> *She is silhouetted halfway against the door, halfway against the wall; nearer the foreground, an older woman, with a great deal of white, which conceals her almost entirely, the shadows full of reflections; white in the shadows.*

Nine years later, in the Salon of 1841, he exhibited a painting entitled, "Jewish Wedding."

After the wedding, the congratulations, the eating, drinking, and dancing, the bride and bridegroom walked out into the night; her white dress turned blue; it grew smaller; finally a speck of dust was blinked away.

On March 11, 1854, Eugene Delacroix sat down at his favorite desk (a gift — actually one of many he had received from a Pasha in Tangiers) and wrote in his journal:

> *A long interruption in these poor notes of daily happenings: I feel very badly about it; these trifling pages written down in such a fugitive way seem to me all that is left of my life, the more it flows away. My lack of memory makes them necessary for me; since the beginning of the year, the steady work needed for finishing at the Hôtel de Ville has been distracting me too much; since I finished it, and that will soon be a month since, my eyes are in a bad state, I am afraid to read and to write.*

He felt as he put down the pen and straightened his back that the rest of his evenings, his nights and days, would be filled with a new kind of darkness. At first he thought he could turn to his friends. But Mme Sand was on her way to Vienna, and Chopin had not received him twice in the last week. Most likely, he was in the throes of composition.

Delacroix felt his fears being heightened by the underlying silence of day becoming night. He wished he were sitting in the green brocade chair in Frederic's apartment, listening to him playing the piano. The evening's shadows, both inside and outside, were beginning to overlap, while he remained seated at his desk, his chin cupped between his hands, his eyes closed.

He remembered that twenty years ago M. Gros had told him that he had once lived a life devoted to excess. But now he, M. Gros, drank nothing but water with dinner. In fact, being deprived of a cigar after dinner was the greatest hardship of all the ones he had to face. Delacroix wondered what he had forgotten about that evening. What moments would never be retrieved?

It was well past midnight, yet restlessness permeated his movements. The moon slit the thick velvet drapes, but it couldn't reach him. Instead, on either side of his bed two strips of light wavered along the carpet. Outside, someone remarked on the sultry beauty of the night in a high silly voice. *I am afraid to read and to write.*

The lamp continued flickering; three dull concentric circles peered back from the ceiling. Delacroix rolled over on his side; he faced the night table, as he had done many times in the last few hours. Except for the table, everything had become a shadow; the chair in the corner was a blotch of darkness. He turned back to the table. A pile of books lay there, precariously balanced. They were a staircase rising in memory of the house that no longer surrounds them.

The Noise of Life

> *The noise of life begins again,*
> *And ghastly through the drizzling rain*
> *On the bald street breaks the blank day.*
> Tennyson, "In Memoriam"

1

One summer they stayed with her family at their cabin; peeling paint, torn and patched screens, doors that never quite closed. It was next to a lake ringed by other such cabins and other such families; afternoons of yelling frolicking yelping wheezing crying sneezing happy bleeding hungry children.

2

Her family: a skinny sister who took long walks in the woods and daydreamed about boys; a skinny brother who daydreamed about being a pilot and flying one of the planes that left a vapor trail over their pond; a skinny father who thought of "projects" for the family to carry out; a round mother who cooked and cheated at cards.

3

The children's room had three lumpy bunk beds and lots of miscellaneous one-of-a-kinds from previous summers: fluffy left slipper; right sandal; bottom of magenta bikini referred to as "the cocktail napkin" (her brother liked dragging out the words, Cock Tail); top of a yellow and white floral patterned two-piece ("looks like bathroom wallpaper"); and four unmatched sneakers. A musty smell, like a jar of cloudy lake water one keeps a crayfish in, invaded everything; shirts socks underpants panties bras nightgown.

4

Around dawn, punctuated by a particularly aggressive woodpecker, she climbed out of the top bunk and slid into his, her nightgown rising as she descended.

"Don't worry. They never wake before I do."

At first he was shy, even afraid. He wondered what it would be like to have an older sister, and to wake one morning and see her fucking her boyfriend. They soon had a common fantasy they never spoke of; they began thrashing and writhing, a little louder each morning, though never talking, just grinning at each other like the idiots they knew themselves to be.

5

One morning he looked solemn (almost ridiculously so, she thought) as he stared into his coffee, while stirring it endlessly, nervously.

"Looking for your nose ring, dearest?"

"I'd like to say that if you have any dreams not to tell me what they were."

"Okay. But why?"

"Because if you tell me your dreams, I won't remember mine."

6

After the fluorescent light in their kitchen burned out, they began cooking with the refrigerator door open. A pale light fanned out over the stove, its circles of blue flame. One afternoon he bought a stronger bulb, in case they ever decided to cook something fancy. Finally, when he couldn't eat Rice Krispies in the morning without thinking of the roaches, he borrowed a ladder from the super and replaced the overhead light. "Snack, Crackle, and Pop," she would yell from the bedroom, when he rifled the refrigerator for a late night snack.

7

When she couldn't find an ashtray, she let the cigarette burn down to the end, and then stood the burnt out filter up in some inconspicuous place. The windowsill was soon filled with orderly rows of charred tan stumps. Also, just under the bed, though a few of them were knocked over when he slid his shoes there. Sometimes, the toilet was flushed twenty-five times a day.

8

One afternoon, while he was at work, she went out and stole a can of pink paint. Standing on a pile of *National Geographics,* which was placed on a chair (the desk was too big to move), she painted a flock of oddly shaped birds across the ceiling and down one wall.

9

"Can I undress you tonight?"
 "No."
 "Why?"
 "Because I'm covered with scales, you toad."

10

They were given: 8 cases of Alaskan Crabmeat (24 cans to a case)
 1 case of ketchup (12 family size bottles)
 3 cans of 5 lb. hams
 2½ cases of canned crepes suzettes (16 cans to a case)
 17 one lb. bags of assorted nuts
 a small vacuum cleaner

Their generous friend (a doctor married to a doctor) explained: "I always buy things in quantity because I don't like to shop. Then, every so often, I have to clean out the pantry because I want to try something else."

For a month they ate crabmeat in every way they could. They went to the library and borrowed piles of cookbooks.

Then they settled for crabmeat omelettes and salads.

Finally, they began eating out.

11

In a more recent *National Geographic* were photographs of two Inca boys that had been found by archaeologists in the Andes. They were perfectly preserved down to their eyes, which were still open and bright. According to the archaeologists, they were an offering to their gods, and had been escorted to their destination above the treeline by their tribe. The boys went willingly, not only because it was a great honor, but also because they had been given a powerful narcotic. They had been sitting and waiting for hundreds of years. He imagined thousands of such boys sitting in their beautifully woven serapes; a community whose citizens were unaware of each other.

12

He threw a gray plastic teacup at her in the middle of an argument. The profusion of apologies did nothing to alter the facts.

13

"Sometimes I think all there is to life is the waiting."
"Yes, but imagine how you can pass the time."

14

They began stealing steaks from the supermarket.

15

On his birthday she cooked him a "surprise" dinner.

It wasn't a flag: it was red, white, and blue:

> chicken breasts with hollandaise sauce
> cream corn dyed red
> mashed potatoes dyed blue

The potatoes looked like a lump of clay. The melting butter didn't help.

Dessert was an angel food cake dyed black.

16

They arranged a meeting in a motel they selected from the Yellow Pages. They both took cabs and arrived an hour late.

17

It was snowing big soft flakes as he returned to the street where they first lived together. He had been walking all afternoon, while she had been interviewing at various agencies, hoping to get a job as a graphics artist. The snow had been pink and red, and now it was blue. It had covered the city in its soft absorbent coat. The cars were wearing mittens. He knew it was coming. A familiar, sneezing, runny-nosed boy was whistling; an arrogant, feigned nonchalance stuck, like the snow, to every shifty gesture. He didn't bother to turn around when the snowball splattered beside him.

18

They looked up at the ceiling, and sometimes he or she would remember the birds.

Toy Trucks and Fried Rice

The Chinese Benevolent Association's Annual Christmas Party was more than high heeled, beehived women in jewelry and satin dresses, men with gold teeth, and bottles of Johnny Walker Red. It was, if anything, a party for their children, and it was held on the first Saturday before Christmas in a banquet-sized room with a stage in the basement of the Chinese Episcopalian Church. There were orderly rows of long picnic tables, white tablecloths, tray after tray of mediocre Chinese restaurant food, and a dozen smiling waiters.

A network of crepe paper stretched across the ceiling. A Christmas tree shone from its corner; at the top of it a silver plated angel smiled benignly over the evening's presents. Beneath the tree were blue duffel bags stuffed with presents. The braver children poked one bag and then another, nearly causing them to topple over. This went on until they were scolded by an openly pleased adult.

Every Christmas party reenacted the previous one down to the smallest detail. Santa Claus, for example, was never Chinese. Instead, he was chosen from among the middle-aged men and women who studied Chinese in a Saturday class held in the church basement. After the dinner was over, these sincere students put on a skit, and sang Christmas Carols in Chinese. After the audience's cheering and clapping subsided, the students walked off the stage and joined the party. Then Santa Claus came out and distributed presents among the elated children.

His parents brought him to the party. He had been told ever since he could remember that he was Chinese. He never lived in Chinatown and he didn't speak a word of Chinese. It was more complicated than that, however. His mother was from Shanghai and spoke the dialect common to that area. The people at the party (he assumed this was true of the students as well) spoke another dialect, Cantonese, and were, according to his mother, only farmers anyway. The analogy his mother made had to do with how people spoke in Louisiana as compared to those in Boston, except that in China they didn't understand each other at all.

The differences were more than just those of language and economics, urban and rural. His mother reminded him that his grandfather was taller than anyone in this room, as were most people from Shanghai. His mother, however, was only a shade above five feet tall, and was thus indistinguishable from the rest of the women in the room.

He had never asked his father if he felt like he was Chinese. He knew his father's mother, an English Catholic, had had him baptized, curled his long hair, and dressed him in girl-like clothes until he was nearly six. He thought of his father's father as a man who was Chinese, but who abandoned all the responsibilities of raising a child to a woman who had wanted a daughter, and was willing for years to pretend she had one. There was another reason for not asking his father. The one thing his father talked to him about, besides World War II, was American history. Every week his father went to the public library and brought home old diaries, documents and studies about the Indians, especially the Sioux, Apaches and Seminoles. They were the fighters his father told him about. His father also told him the Indians were the only true Americans and everyone else was a fake.

His mother had grown up in a 27 room house on Great Western Way. Her father had been the Ambassador to Belgium in Sun-Yat Sen's doomed republic. Private tutors came and left her room at their appointed hour. Most of the time this narrative of sumptuousness didn't surface as an ironic commentary on the present. However, when the exceptions did occur, it was because she was thrown irretrievably into the past, as at this party. She tried to convey to her son the belief that isolation, whether social or spiritual, was the inevitable result of being better than what was around you. It was one of the ways she comforted herself.

At another table a smooth faced man wipes his chopsticks with a napkin. A mother cleans off the tines of each fork before handing it to her children. He remembers that his mother methodically cleans off the inside rim of a can after opening it, and before emptying the contents into a pot. She had to learn how to cook when she came to America.

They lived in one room of a boarding house in a mill town north of Boston. They moved when she saw another boarder pissing in the sink, instead of waiting to use the bathroom.

A young woman in a turquoise satin dress walked across the room until she reached a table where a young man put out his cigarette and stood up to greet her. A young girl smiled and clapped her hands, as her father tore off the bright wrapping paper. Toy trucks and cars bumped into the half empty plates of food.

He scans the room, looks at his plate, goes back to staring at the young woman.

Late one night, an old friend of his mother came to visit. They always spoke in their native dialect when they were together. The friend said she couldn't find a parking space so she had put the helicopter on the roof. She hoped nobody would mind. Had he understood her correctly? Maybe he was mistaken? He couldn't wait until she left to find out, so he asked his mother if he could go out. His mother smiled and said of course. He sat on the curb across the street. The living room light was the only light on in the house. He could see his mother and her friend talking and smiling. To anyone else it might have looked like they were exchanging recipes, or looking through snapshots from a picnic they had gone on last summer.

An old woman in a brown pleated cotton coat carefully picked her way among the children, occasionally stopping to pinch their cheeks and smile. Her face was made up of deep lines, as if it was being folded smaller and smaller.

Before eating, everyone bowed their heads and said grace. Father Kwo stood up at the head table and made his blessing in both Chinese and American. The talking resumed. His suit felt too tight. He sat in a metal chair and listened to a language neither he nor his parents could understand. All around them was bright embroidered satin, a kind of tinsel he will be attracted to for years.

Electric Drills

I used to have a fear of tools, largely because of my father. When I was three, and he, my mother, and I lived in a basement apartment on Beacon Hill, my father developed a ritual to scare me when I misbehaved. Somewhere, he had acquired a beautiful set of tools, each of them red and shiny like a child's fire truck. I don't know why or where he got them, since I have never seen him use them again. I remember the apartment as industrial green. There were lots of pipes overhead, and linoleum seems to have been on all the floors. I also remember the high chair, and the arm chair I had to sit in when my father was mad at me. It faced the closet. While I was sitting there, feeling smaller than I should have in this chair for adults, my father would get out the electric drill, plug it in, and open the closet door until I could see both him and it in profile. He would then drill some holes in the door, while telling me I had been "bad," and the possible consequences that might result if I continued to misbehave. The insistence of his voice competing with the whining of the electric drill was always what frightened me the most.

Eighteen years later, when I was a student at Bard College, I got into a car accident. I was admitted to Northern Dutchess Hospital on May 29th, 1971 and left for the first time on January 15th, 1972. I had forty-seven roommates, and watched two of them die. There were four of us in the car, a baby blue '65 Chevy, we had borrowed from a friend who had passed out on the floor of his room, after extolling the poems of Pushkin in Russian. I bent down, took the keys from his pocket, flipped them in the air, and said to the other three in my best Randolph Scott–James Dean voice—"Let's go for a ride."

At the time of the accident, the two with driver's licenses were sitting in the back. The one who was driving, had never driven before, and hasn't since. The car hit a tree head on. I was lying under the car, near the rear wheel, when I regained consciousness. Both my legs (right tibia, left femur) were broken, as well as my pelvis and nose. I required stitches in my mouth and on my face. My right ring finger was dislocated. I was awake for most of the operation, since the amount of liquor and drugs I had taken eliminated the possibility of anesthesia. While I was lying in the Pre-Op room, they began giving me morphine to ease the pain.

For most of the time, when I was under morphine, I felt like America while a lot of riots were taking place in Canada. I knew it was going on, but I didn't particularly care. I tore out my stitches, undid my bandages, ripped the tubes for the plasma and glucose out of my arms, and called the nurses names that, as one of them said with a smile months later, she didn't know existed. I don't remember any of these things, since they all took place at night, and I was supposedly asleep. Eventually, I would light my bed on fire because, as I told my roommate, I wanted to see what it was like. The morphine was then discontinued, though I would be given it for five more periods, each lasting up to a week, and I would refine the possibilities of how I felt with liquor, grass, and valiums I had saved up.

When the doctors set my right leg, I remember feeling the warmth of the plaster-soaked bandage, and being surprised. It felt invigorating, and I told the doctors they "should set the rest of me like that." I don't remember the whine of the electric drill as much as the realization that something horrible was happening to me. I was tied to the operating table's cold narrow slab. I managed to sit up and see one of the doctors drilling through my left leg, just below the knee. The drill was green, like the living room of the apartment on Beacon Hill. The pin would remain there, attached to weights, nearly the whole time I was in the hospital. I was taken out of traction when the decision was made to put a stainless steel plate in my left leg, from my hip to just above my knee. The doctor showed me the plate in a catalog that reminded me of Sears. Beneath the picture was a list of its vital dimensions. They probably used a drill to attach it to my femur, which, as the doctors said, "looked like a stack of marbles." A month later the doctors inserted two pins into my right leg, after resetting it. It seems that it hadn't been done correctly on that first morning.

A couple of months after I got out of the hospital, I was sitting in Adolph's, the Bard campus bar, drinking with a friend. I had been thinking of electric drills, and the part they played in my life—both in the psychological development and the physical reconstruction of my body. At that point, I had not yet moved to Manhattan, bought a loft, and built a lot of bookcases and furniture—all with a gray electric drill I had bought as a gift for the sculptor I was living with. According to my friend, I had a bemused smile on my face when I turned to him and said, "Do you want to hear a funny story?" Recently, I called him up. We haven't seen much of each other in the last seven years, but we manage to keep in touch. He asked me if I ever thought about writing down the story I told him.

The Telephone Call

He was my third roommate. We were together for twenty-four hours. The first one, Mr. Pell, was eventually moved to another room because he had managed to completely unnerve me within three days. At first, I thought I was going crazy, but the doctor, in attempt to reassure me, said he was "a real case." He wore maroon corduroy pajamas, was nearly seventy, bald, and had glasses perched on a beak-like nose, giving him a predatory look. On the first morning, after putting on his pajamas, he wiggled his hips and asked me if he looked like Elvis Presley.

He used to move my water glass beyond my reach, and then pretend not to hear me when I asked him if he could get it for me. I had gone through the windshield of a car, and was in double traction. He told me I looked awful, and then hovered over my bed with a small pocket mirror. He said I would definitely need plastic surgery, and that I would "probably never look the same again." He also told his wife he had lived a good honest life and was ready. I knew there was nothing wrong with him, because the doctor had just told him he was "as fit as a fiddle." I watched his wife weeping, as he nonchalantly turned the pages of his newspaper, and wished he would drop dead right then and there.

My second roommate, Mr. Bouton, was a thirty-two year old tree surgeon. His wife Irma, a few years younger than John, visited him every day. He had ulcers, and was there for two months because something had gone wrong after the operation. A clear plastic tube was inserted through each nostril to drain the blood from the operation and prevent infection. The tubes emptied into a bottle that looked like a five gallon pickle jar.

He was given Demerol, a slightly milder pain killer than morphine. He once got out of bed and began dragging it and the bottle across the floor. I remember waking up and hearing him say: "Let's go to town, get two quarts of LSD and some girls."

John and Irma were married while still in high school. They had four children, the oldest was fifteen and the youngest four. Six months later, Irma would come into the hospital, have her fifth child, a boy, and get her tubes tied. Two years later, I would bump into him in the Grand Union in Rhinebeck, New York. He still had his quiet smile, and it still frightened me, since he seemed more desperate than he was letting on. Recently, I was reminded of him when a friend read a line from Auden about not giving a gun to a melancholic bore.

I had been in Northern Dutchess Hospital for sixty-five days, when the nurses decided to move my bed next to the window. Since I was confined to the bed, its location was important to me. In my new position the room seemed larger because I could see anyone passing in the hall. I also could look out the window at the trees on the other side of the parking lot, the people coming to visit the hospital walking up the little walkway, and the progress of a building that was being constructed. But the most important thing about being near the window was the sky. Especially at night.

Around 3:00 pm, on August 3rd, 1971, in Rhinebeck, New York, it was gray. "I am in the hospital, thinking of hospitals. The gray sky reminds me of being sick, and staying inside." On August 3rd, 1971, I wrote this without any sense of irony. I was 21, and I wanted to be a writer.

The second time I thought I was going crazy, I was in a mildly dreamy state from morphine, and was gazing out the window. Two World War I biplanes flew by, either Spads or Sopwith Camels. They were being chased by two bright red German biplanes. A few disconcerting moments passed before I remembered the Rhinebeck Aerodrome was nearby, and, all summer long, antique airplane buffs put on shows of this sort. The oddest thing about this experience was that they never flew past my window again. Often I would wonder if what I was hearing was the churning monotony of their engines signaling the fact that they would soon be flying past my window.

Moving me from one side of the room to the other was

something of a social event. It took six nurses to move the unwieldy bed. They also had to move all my books, the urinal and bed pan, and a few bottles of liquor. The last thing they moved was a friend's painting. For a while it was somewhat embarrassing to the nurses, as well as to the hospital, since it was a nude. It had been painted in a way reminiscent of Renoir, full of fleshy pinks, bright and airy. I used to wait and see how my roommates, their wives, and children would react to it. All of them were obvious. No one ever mentioned how badly it had been painted.

There was also a new nurse on the afternoon shift, Mrs. Costello, a thirty year old, dark haired Italian woman, lithe with cat-like eyes, who said she had been writing poetry for seventeen years. Her favorite poets were Kahlil Gibran and Walt Whitman. She would later become a nurse at the Bard College Infirmary, and I once contemplated pretending to be sick so I could watch her hover over me.

His name was Art Blauvelt. I have never been sure how to spell his name, and every time I think of him, I also think of the James Bond movie, *The Man with the Golden Gun.* The evil character in the movie is named "Blauvelt," and lives on an impregnable island off the coast of China. I don't know what Art did for a living. He was married and had at least one daughter. She was in her early twenties and married to a cop in St. Louis.

Art was forty-seven, and had had four heart attacks in nine years. He was brought into my room from the Intensive Care Unit, which was directly across the hall. The nurses placed what looked like an elongated traveling case for pets over his legs, so that nothing would be touching them.

Periodically, Art was given shots of Heperin, which is an anti-coagulant often given to patients with heart trouble. I could tell from the tones of their voices that the doctors and nurses were worried. If a blood clot developed in the legs, it would move to the heart. "Flipped an embolism" is a term I heard used in another case. This is probably what happened, though I never asked the doctor.

It was nearly sunset. His wife, a tall gentle gray haired woman, talked to me for a while, then turned to her husband and said: "Some people have it worse than you, Art." She seemed neither prodding nor condescending to either of us when she said this. Art's first roommate, a young blond man who had lost two of his toes in a farming accident, later told me she used to bring them both the Sunday paper. On the first Sunday after Art died, she brought him the paper, squeezed his hand, and left without saying a word.

We talked all night. He kept apologizing because he couldn't reach the call button to get the nurses. He kept shitting in his bed, and having to have the nurses change the sheets. They always came very quickly, and I could tell they liked him a lot by the way they reassured him. He told me he had taken up knitting in the hospital, and that each thing he had made (sweaters, Afghans) he had given to the nurses to use.

"At times flashes hit me that I am in the hospital. Usually the flash originates from another patient."

I remember telling you my roommate died while we were talking on the phone. I hadn't said anything at the time, though I could hear Art pleading with his wife to get the nurses, because there was nothing you could do. I was surprised when I said that to you, because, up until that moment, I hadn't been conscious of what it was I was thinking when I picked up the phone and dialed, except that I hoped you were there.

BROKEN OFF BY THE MUSIC
(1981)

Scenes from the Life of Boullee

1

Roof shaped like a strawberry. Hurriedly torn
paper towel. The queen's staircase does not
lead to the king's chambers. The traditional
requirements of comfort and convenience.
A kind of sleepwalking echoed by a line
in history. Stands on a lovesick giant
and calls himself a hero. Sound of annoyance
at an unforeseen circumstance becoming an
inevitable consequence. Wine dripping off
the formica table onto the shag rug after
hitting the unused wooden chair covered
with cigarette burns. A dream heard
second hand. An extra coat hanger.
Only half the story is true. The rest
is necessary, like clouds on a cloudy day.

2

Pieces of a piece. The face in the window larger
than the window facing in. A mermaid selling
cheese in a laundromat in Ottawa. A cop who looks
as if he has to go to the bathroom. A bony hand
dangling from a red station wagon. Riding in a cab
with a junkie who wants an alarm clock. Breaking
a promise and counting the pieces. Her harsh
lipstick crumbling over her harsher smile.
Remnants of a collision in a galaxy whose
name is a number. Eeriness of a city with
only one light. The kinds of certainty
available in a drugstore. Jumbo food.
With only one light on. A junkie dangling
from an alarm clock. Using the laundromat
because there are no bathrooms around.
Stealing the mermaid's cheese. Breaking
into her smile. The kinds of certainty
available in a supermarket, a newspaper,
a lover. A young cop who looks as if he
has gone. The square face in the round
window. Pieces of a blue piece.

3

Without noticing the fire descending into the
subway station. Descending into the copper
sunlight. Going back again and again.
Their voices. One dripping. The other dribbling
to a stop. Lengthening each of the sounds into
a staircase. I think there's three volumes.
A salmon. A sale's on. Ceylon. Existence
being the only record of their names.
Shoes seen by the side of the highway
leading to Las Vegas. Faces remembered
from last Thursday. Talking to an imaginary
friend in your sleep. Waking up and feeling
the sweat. The sweet surrounding your skin.
Adding to the pile. The only thing invisible
for miles. In every kind of light. The light
of topless dancing. Only half of you is there.
No music sparring with traffic. Enters
in a suit the color of coffee, face the color
of masking tape. Everyone looks like you, today.
Even people I don't like.

4

A room with open windows facing a street
where dogs gather at night. Falling curtain.
Refrigerator whose parts can't be replaced.
A full garbage bag waiting for someone by not
waiting for anything. Smoke on a horizon that
exists as a footnote. Unable to see all of
the sky all at once, how the city breaks it
into the pieces needed to cross the street.
Ridden speechless. Frogs frozen under the
curving black marble table. Nothing closer
than the next smile to break the back of
the king. Residential talons. An ashtray
full of rubber bands. Happy with his
gladiatorial entertainment. Happy
with the smoke blocking out the sun.
When a place becomes a person
whose place it is.

5

The rising cost of heart attacks. Different colored bricks in a brick wall. The milky water caused by adding a lemon. The need for second hand pace makers. A fantastic throne of irresponsibility. Names being their only existence. Smell of clean laundry. Sound of ginger ale bubbling inside a can. Sound of irresponsibility. Smell of their names being the only record of their existence. The need for second hand bricks. Piece of yellowing scotch tape peeling off the cabinet door. Largest incision possible. Adding a roof.

6

Zebra-striped pillow. The restlessness
of the jungle in a bed of poses. Not
what he had in mind, but what he had.
The rising cost of platitudes. Why
these questions, these answers, these
beginnings whose endings sail off into
familiar cliches. Suburbs of Samarkand.
Roof shaped like a milk carton. Dormer
window whose mystery was never resolved.
You can't judge a library by its cover.
Broken by the sand, the slipping away
on a shore not bound by the water.

7

Realizing that any certainty is an old one.
The difference between their similarities.
On the back alleys of cities whose avenues
are lushly described adventures. False starts.
Gleam of a cabin cruiser at night in a new
and otherwise empty parking lot. The round
caution with which she danced. The kind of
precociousness found only in octogenarians.

8

So much of the proscenium burned
away by its own curving pride.
Broken by the law of averages.
Toward the moonlight slipping down
the banyan leaves. Characterized
by an earlobe. Under the twitching
grin was an often neglected acumen.
The clouds act like clouds. Snuggling
weather. Like a rope dangling from
a tree, a site where there is
more conjecture than hard knowledge.

9

Rubbing her sable with long thoughtful
fingers. Skimming the curdles of the dream.
His eyes, dull and tired, like grape seeds.
Gravy stains from the previous tenant.
Motif clouds. A summer shaped like
a hot dog, and its rungs of sunlight.
Nails—no two bent the same way.

10

The stumbling blocks are realigned
until a dome appears. After the lake
loses its flag of nervousness. A
parlor-like garage full of bicycles
and unmuddy children. A lemonade-colored
star. Nodding to the famous twins
sitting in opposite windows. Crossing
the river while the sun is about to set
like a mustache on a windowsill. But
it is a happiness without pleasure.

11

The sheets dangling from the line,
smudged photographs of snow.
A rising cenotaph of moonlight.
Surrounded by photographs of prosperity.
Quivering as if the birds had just left.
Sound of ginger ale bubbling inside
a bottle. Undistinguished except by this
reminder, this hurricane in an apple tree.

12

A casual solitude that is beyond casualness.
The snow braids its crumbling ladders.
A smudge of her smile remained on his cheek.
Surely, the wind will reach us, someday,
when the curtains have been drawn back
into their folds. Is it like knowing that
a clock is always surrounded by time?
They took luck to mean an accident which
benefitted them all. The island still
presents a number of problems, though none
of them are as overwhelming as the rain
trickling down the walls. Then I wake up
and begin driving.

13

Counting the times as if they added up.
A haze flattens the city into a blackboard
that needs washing. The grime remaining.
The grim remains. Leaning against
an attitude out of fear. The cane of
canes. Bearing dignified fronts,
proud of them as they are of well-behaved
children. After losing the lorgnettes
in the taxi, their second afternoon
together was as round as a teacup.
The sound of their shovels eroding
into doubt. Watched their daughter
crying in a field, while the sky
unfurled its glistening poncho.

14

Stuffing yourself into a blizzard.
The heavy brass knocker in the form
of a laugh. The passageway leading
from the living room to the study
became a memory of other possibilities.
Red piano keys of sunset.
On a motorcycle beside a wheel
larger than you. On one
corner of a porch were two
coffee cups full of rainwater
and dust. The rope that might
have once restrained a dog.
Counting her gray hairs in the
blue mirror of the polished linoleum.
A barbarian surprise reached the gates
of the kingdom. The light shifted among
the leaves, like a rat. Skirted the edge
of her smile. Another autobiography
sinking beneath its glittering reflections.
The sky hopes to find a new purpose, while
hints of snow left a stain on every collar.

15

The scotch tape scars on the wall. Scared
as a gorilla in a parachute. The moon
might be right on schedule, but the play
is over. Especially as the night remains
at our side, like a finger held up to
the lips. The headlights form an echo
around their glistening chrome. In the
window of the burned-out drugstore.
In the lengthening shadows
of the strawberry-colored roof.

16

The certainty of being part of the atmosphere
is also an aspirin. The desire to listen to
the cement of emotions as opposed to its
bricks. The various formats of disgrace,
and their subheadings, was one way he
avoiding going to the store. The world
of institutions beside the institutions
of the world. The bartered bride is an opera,
but the battered bride is not singing.
The perfection of greed as a sign of the times.

Late Night Movies I

In a small underground laboratory the brain of a
movie actor is replaced by semi-precious stones,
each one thought to have once resided in heaven.

An archaeologist realized the inside of an ancient
mask carried a picture of satin meant only for its
dead inhabitant. A nurse walked into a hospital
and knew something was missing.

In the afternoon, rain washed away all traces
of the railroad station. A crow hid its head
under its wing. A tourist sneezed twice and
wondered if there was any truth to the legend
inscribed over the doorway of the pharmacy.

Beware the opinions of a dead movie actor,
an empty hospital and a wounded crow
        on a rainy afternoon,
a missing brain and a train station built beside a river,
a nurse carrying a photograph of heaven.

In a small laboratory in heaven the semi-precious thoughts
of a movie actor are replaced by a brain.
The ancient mask realized the insides of the
archaeologist exuded a tincture of *Pisa*
meant only for its dead inhabitant.

Outside the train station the nurse wondered if
there was any truth to the legend inscribed

around the rims of her new tires. The brain
of the movie actor is carried by a tourist
from one day to the next.

In a small underground temple the wing of a crow
is replaced by semi-precious stones, each one
thought to have been a sneeze from heaven.

The nurse hid the hands of Orpheus under a painting
of a train station, whose shadows reached the river
where all legends began. A doctor realized the
doorway of the pharmacy was missing. A woman
wondered why a picture of heaven had replaced
her tires.

The movie actor's only desire was to be seen
by the dead, to be fixed in the lining
of the clouds over their graves.

The archaeologist slept in a hospital with
as many windows as days in the year and wondered
if there was any truth to the legend inscribed
on the semi-precious stones the tourist carried
across the plaza in the afternoon rain.

At times, the nurse thought the only desires
were the ones without names.

The head of Orpheus floated down the river, leaving
behind the hospital, where, as one version
of the legend claimed, the song would continue
forever in the hallways leading to the sea.

Late Night Movies II

Gone with the wind. What remains of the charred
tool box is something the detective cannot get
off his mind.

Through the dirty window, down an alley strewn with
identifiable pieces of garbage, toward the doorway
of a rundown hotel. Bits fly back.

Snores rise through the rafters of the sagging barn.
The creature crawls out of the swamp, and begins
walking around the campfire. Introduces a blonde,
a smile, and a promise.

Done with the wing. He cannot scrape the detective's
charred remains off the tool box. The blonde smiles,
combs her hair, and then lights a cigarette in the
deserted bus station. Identifiable pieces
of the creature fly back through the dirty window.

An itch in time staves nine. The blonde smiles,
combs her cigarette, and then lights her
sagging swamp on fire. What remains of the
detective crawls past the dirty window.

Stalk walls and carry a big tick. Perhaps
the creature will turn in time to keep his
throat intact, his snores identifiable.

The bomb continues its countdown in an aisle.
A child opens his hand over and over. What
remains of the tool box rises through
the rafters of a sagging hotel.
Introduces a snore, crawls out of a smile,
scrapes an itch, combs the throat.

Don't wire until you see the fights of their eyes.
Introduced in the doorway of a hotel. Pine tree
moonlight. Tonight, a bird in the band is worth
two in the hush; the hush surrounding
a lifetime of guarantees.

Late Night Movies III

1

The head man did the right thing. He displayed
his wit, as they watched the snow from a bench
in the park. However, when the weather cleared,
Rimbaud knew his boss would order the dogs to
continue hauling the men to paradise.

The dead man hid the right thing. He displayed
his bit, as they snatched the woe from a wench
in the park. However, when the weather cleared,
Baudelaire knew his boss would order the dogs to
continue mauling the hen to paradise.

2

Rimbaud was alone when he picked up the tongs
and stood by the side of the river. A bad planner,
he carried his first marriage into the mountains,
where she would burn his toast to ashes every
morning. But tonight, during the late night movies,
he listened for the hush coming from the gate.

Baudelaire was alone when he picked up the songs
and stood by the tide of the river. A plaid banner.
He married his first carriage into the mountains,
where she would turn his boast to ashes every
morning. And tonight, during the mate night lovies,
he heard the gush coming from the hate.

3

In the market place Rimbaud watched and followed
them. An old man and his wife wanted their son
to trade for gold. All the wheat they harvested
for a tiny bag of radiant specks. By the end of
the afternoon both of them were hurrying in front
of the waiting salesman.

In the market place Baudelaire watched and followed
them. An old man and his wife wanted to trade their son
for gold. All the heat they saved had harvested
this tiny radiant speck. By the end of the afternoon,
however, both of them were worrying in front
of the hating salesman.

4

After he left the mountain fired with autumn,
Rimbaud preferred sleeping in a corner of the
library, and, later, washing his hands in the
park. He was tired of unloading baskets of
canned meat for the butchers of Toledo.
When it rains, it pours, he thought. And
he wanted to move up to sardines and crumbs.

After he left the fountain mired with autumn,
Baudelaire preferred weeping in the corner of the
library, and, later, slashing his hands in the
park. He was tired of unloading caskets of
banned meat for the butchers of Toledo.
When it pains, it roars, he thought. And
he wanted to arrive with carbines and drums.

5

The rain began pushing him back into the hospital.
After months of washing their dirty dishes, Rimbaud

knew he had to leave this infernal house of death,
or perish. The skies had cleared, but there was
still a sense of doom in the air, as he glanced
out the open window, hoping the next time he would
        leave forever.

The pain began pushing him back into the hospital.
After months of dashing their dirty dishes, Baudelaire
knew he had to heave this infernal louse of death,
or perish. The skies had cleared, but there was
still a sense of gloom in the air, as he danced
out the open window, hoping the next time he would
        leave forever.

Late Night Movies IV

All that remains of the garden is the shadow
it casts on the wall surrounding the palace.

At night the priest takes the mask out of the fire.
According to the local weather bureau it was going
to be another long day, full of surprises. Inside
her room the queen prayed for an artist who could
engrave her portrait on the surface of the moon.

Only the stars can engrave their shadows
onto the sleep of the king, the last one
        told her.
Only the sound of blood dripping from
a severed hand onto newspapers can awaken him.
Only the voice of his dead sister can comfort him.

All that remains of the fruit truck is the apple.
One by one the boys line up. Just before dawn
the priest leaves the hut and makes a task out of
the fire; the fire still warm enough to dance in.

All that remains of the garden are echoes
of the dead sister. According to the writing of her
        severed hand
the newspapers are full of surprising errors.
At night the dogs line up and wait to use
the wall surrounding the palace.

Just before noon the priest of the weather
bureau walks through the palace looking for
a phone booth. According to the king it is
going to be another long prediction. Only
the sound of gasoline dripping from a fruit
truck can comfort him. Only the echo of rain
can make him speak.

If only the priest could cast his predictions
into the restless sleep of the king.
If only the newspapers could counsel him
in ways to return dance to the kingdom.
If only the shadow of the ziggurat did not
fall across his wish to know how long it took
for the day to end up where it began.

According to the blind queen, memory is the voice
of someone dead.

The way the garden stirred ever so slightly
reminded him of conversations he had had
with the other guards—its wind among the leaves.

All that remains of the shadow is the wall
        it once engraved.

Shanghai Shenanigans

The moon empties its cigarette over a row of clouds
whose windowsills tremble in the breeze

The breeze pushed my boat through a series
of telephone conversations started by perfume

Perfume splashed over the words of a nomad
who believed it was better to starve than to laugh

To laugh at the administration's most recent mishap
will make the guests stay until the party

Until the party is bundled in chatter
I will count the pearls lingering around your neck

Rumors

At the beginning of a street some say never ends
is a statue whose inscription says otherwise.

Some rivers remain questions, shifting
from side to side. Other questions
remain rivers, thick and muddy.
One bridge is a moth-eaten highway.
Another is a rhinestone bridge.

An architect wants to build a house
rivaling the mountains surrounding
his sleep, each turret mute as a hat.
He crosses a river to reach ground
hard enough to begin his plan.
He crosses a river the way
a river crosses his sleep,
swirling with questions.

The inscription says the river flows back
into the mountains carrying the dead.
Silver coins on their eyes. Silver coins
engraved with the faces of those left behind.
On squealing streets. On pavements
rippling beneath a pyramid of glances.

At the beginning of the street some say never ends
is a river curving beneath the city, carrying
the architect to sleep. Every morning

the clouds resemble something more terrifying,
until all resemblance ends, and he wakes up
in an empty hall, alone on a river.

The Dream Life of a Coffin Factory in Lynn, Massachusetts

Earlier in the century it was not unusual to spend an evening
      on the verandah.
It was a time when movie theaters sprawled around
newly constructed lagoons, their blue concrete walls
rising out of Wisconsin snow drifts, their tile roofs
fiercely gathering Delaware's wind-swept soot in March.

Every street personalized its drugstore with mahogany stools
on which one could perch, and wait for evening to unfold its
      newspaper, shake out its umbrella.
And at night, long after everyone was asleep,
the rows of chrome spigots still glistened with pride.

Now it was dusk; and floating above these warm suburbs
was a tremendous dome, whose perimeter was molded
with high relief figures of motorcycles and pouting dancers,
wagon wheels and other things classical.

In Wisconsin's lagoons it was still considered graceful
for a man to sit in a drugstore and wait for a hand
      to squeeze an orange pill.

In Delaware's soot a woman could sit on a wall
and lose hours counting clouds unfolding
      in the darkness.

It was, if anything, a newly constructed century—
a time when only motorcycles sprawled fiercely
      in the rain.

Behind the movie theater a warm glow spread out
from the window of the hacienda, bravely gathering
the remnants of evening to its yellow handkerchief.

Even the narrower streets had their own lagoons,
each one lined with stucco clouds on which one could sleep,
waiting for evening to deliver its pastel uniforms.
It would remain an evening of waiting,
for men and women floated above the suburbs,
pouting fiercely in the last stages of a withered century.

In March, in Wisconsin, young men shed their mustaches.
        After carefully weighing them,
they were placed in linen handkerchiefs and buried in the snow.
In the evening they ran back to the classical suburbs,
where rows of young women leaned in glistening drugstores,
waiting for the clouds to get older.

The perimeter of these suburbs was carefully outlined
        by chrome spigots.
Lawns rose fiercely out of the snow, while paper bags
        seldom crossed the avenue.
If a newspaper floated past a window, a pale hand clutched
        a withered foot.
It was a time when the century had gone to sleep,
and everyone glistened with pride.

Avenue of Americans

The audience cheers as the monkey correctly
identifies their desire by curling his lips
around the statue of a cigarette.
Stretching from knee to shiny knee,
somehow it made sense.
Nurses attended to his every skid.
She woke up, remembering the miles of empty sky
unfurling from banner to banner.

The woman skidded to a halt when she saw a monkey
climb onto her windshield with a letter clamped
        firmly in his mouth.
The plane stretched beside the mountain,
its seats bubbling with cheers that faded
only as night demanded its portion of the rent.
The highway leading to the statue's permanent shrug.

The monkeys arranged themselves in alphabetical order.
To convert failure into success, the president was advised
to stop scratching his nose with his thumb.
She woke up and was rewarded
with questions leading to questions.

Each street is named after a country
that does not return its mail.
The president of the monkeys corrected his audience
by adjusting his smile from moment to moment.
Permanent shrug of her cigarette.

Inside the letter was the map of the highway
leading to the correct audience.
A response is not necessarily an answer.
Minutes arrange themselves in a circular alphabet;
statue first, shrug second.
Success was as simple.
But whose angel was perched on the smiling monkey's shoulder?

> His hand held all the answers to some of the questions.
> I learned to accommodate your doubts by lying.
>
> His answers held hands with some of the questions.
> I learned to accommodate myself by doubting my own lies.

The president's smile faded only when it made sense.
On the bus, the monkey sat next to a man smoking a pipe.

Each street is named after a shrug.

The highway fades into the side of a night scarred by mountains.
The echo of the president's smile is carried from promise to
    promise.
The boy hides the answers in his mouth, his elbows scratching his
    knees.
If he is lucky, amnesia will be his reward.

A Different Cereal

The moon shrinks behind a row of shriveled trees.
An empty parking lot, a man reading a newspaper
        inside an illuminated box.
After reaching into the cupboard, her hand closed
its five fingers around a leatherbound volume.
Later, the aspirin would not dissolve in a spoon of water.

An empty parking lot sinks behind a man
reading a leatherbound volume of fingernails.
Reaches for an illuminated cereal box, teeth closing.
Later, behind a row of trivial shrieks, the car would not start.
Inside the envelope were three blue stars, the dead general's
    photograph.

After relieving the television of its promises,
she reaches for her illuminated fingernails,
while he sinks the rest of his teeth
into the leatherbound cereal box.
Beside the orange, an envelope
with three blue spoons painted on its flap.

The general quickly dissolved into a shriveled cereal,
his fingers scratching an empty box of illuminated shrieks.
Later, beneath the rows of parking stars, a man
grinds an aspirin into the cement.
When the wind ripped the leaves from the trees,
it was as if murder slid out of the swamp.

After licking rows of stamps
she stood behind a tree.
He wanted to know why his car would not relieve him
of the headaches of television.
Eventually, the moon is replaced by a picture of trees,
each ripped from the leaves of a leatherbound volume.

The dead general wrote to his mother
asking her to send a different cereal.
The doctor's ashes were spooned into an envelope
and mailed to a woman who reads newspapers in a car.

Smiles broke the ice that formed along
the rows of fingernails illuminated by the moon.
A box of shrieks was delivered to a television station.
After circling the tree four times, the general's dog
placed the envelope inside the cereal box.

She watched the cars inching back and forth
        across her television.
Stands behind a smile, a handshake, a newspaper.
Eventually, the swamp will reach the gates of the parking lot,
where the shadows of the living mix with the dust of the dead.

After carefully opening each letter,
she placed the shrieks in a leatherbound volume.
She liked the way they illuminated the parking lot
when the wind ripped her sighs to shreds.

Gloves removed the hands
and placed them beside
the newspaper.

Turned to the smile that worked best beneath the moon.
Crack of a whip, wrack of a crib.
Enough that inside the envelope
        was the cereal
the children have been shrieking for.

Broken Off by the Music

With the first gray light of dawn
the remnants of gas stations and supermarkets
assume their former shapes.

A freckled, red headed boy stares into the refrigerator,
its chrome shelves lined with jars, cans, and bottles—
each appropriately labeled with a word and a picture.

For some of the other inhabitants of the yellow apartment house,
the mere vapor of food in the morning is sufficient nourishment.

Along the highway
dozens of motorists have pulled onto the shoulder of the road,
no longer guided by the flicker of countless stars
dancing over the surface of the asphalt.
Three radios disagree over what lies ahead.
It is morning, and sand no longer trickles
onto the austere boulevards of the capital.

Outside, on the sidewalk,
two young girls kneel down and pray
in front of a restaurant closed for vacation.
A breeze reminds everyone that ice is another jewel—
the result of snow gleaming at night.
"I used to play on this street, but now it is different,"
      says the older girl.
The younger one, who might be her sister, nods solemnly.
Across the street is a store no one will enter.

Distance can hardly lend enchantment
to the remnants of a supermarket
where faces are torn, as always,
between necessity and desire.

With the first gray light of evening
a freckled girl assumes her former shape—
each limb appropriately labeled with words of instruction.

The younger boy skips away from the others,
while singing a song full of words he stumbles over.

Outside the capital,
two motorists disagree over the remnants of a refrigerator.
Three boys stare at what lies behind the stars.
A breeze reminds everyone of their former shapes,
while evening lends austere enchantment
to the yellow window of a gas station.

Snow can hardly lend enchantment to a sidewalk
where two young girls shiver uncontrollably,
while looking for the doorway of a store that is closed.
Nearby, a woman labels gray shapes with songs of disagreement.

Three supermarkets disagree over food vapors in a refrigerator.
Along the highway sand becomes a song of chrome enchantment.
A young boy kicks the remnants of his brother's radio.
"I used to pray on this street, but now it is sufficient to return,"
      he whispers,
as if someone is listening.

A woman stops in front of the gas station and stares
at the surface of the stars drifting through the clouds.

The breeze reminds the motorist
that the first gray light of dawn
is the remnant of a jewel.

Thousands of radios begin flickering
throughout the apartment complex.

The shoulders of the younger sister are covered with snow.
The sidewalk in front of the restaurant is littered
with sleeping motorists, each of them staring
at the breeze trickling from the clouds.
But at night, the sky is a window full of earrings,
each lost in its blue velvet box.

Two boys nod solemnly in front of their former shapes.
Someone has embroidered the remnants of sufficient enchantment.

CORPSE AND MIRROR
(1983)

Two Kinds of Song

It is said the palace was modeled on a dream, but even what the king remembers of his dream is not necessarily the dream itself. Will this space between the pages of sleep and the writing of day always exist? I do not know. I might never know. I am only a guard—a fixture that moves like the polished hands of a clock.

It is said there is nothing about your life the king does not know. All of the halls surrounding his private chambers are painted blue to remind us how the sky, where he and the gods converse nightly, lies forever beyond our reach. Today, from the tower, I watched the clouds scurrying overhead. They were in a tizzy, like newlyweds shopping in the marketplace. Maybe the priests are right. Maybe the king does know what I am thinking, for even my metaphors defeat me.

Now, the only glimpse of hope I have is when I am assigned to the corridor where the stately rows of deities smile at me from their dusty niches. When I am near them I feel something is askew, that the dream was remembered incorrectly, and these statues, these material echoes of the invisible, know more than they are saying, even to the king. And, at dawn, as I return to the barracks to sleep, I hear the birds singing in the palace garden, singing as if their song was meant only for the deaf.

Missing Pages

From the balcony of the seaside hotel you can see the jeweled towers rising from the bay's seemingly calm waters. Some say they are the remnants of an ancient port, the survivors of an earthquake. But it seems unlikely such a rupture in the earth's mantle would leave these edifices behind, each of them as bright and unmarred as it was on the morning the masons and priests dismantled the scaffolding, and stood back to see what had been accomplished in obdurate stone.

By the second morning of our visit, these symbols of the miraculous are the axis around which all our routines revolve. Our meals are eaten on the balcony, or by the window when it rains. Inevitably, our walks end up at the edge of the pier. And, on the one morning they were shrouded in fog, we shuffled aimlessly through the hotel corridors, unable to do anything but commiserate with each other over their absence.

The one fact that saved us, of course, was the realization we were guests on this island. But for the people living here it must be very different. Each of us has wondered why they do not question the presence of these towers glowing offshore on the nights the moon anchors its orange boat above the harbor. The band continues playing its repertoire of favorite tunes, and the bartender tells the same stories about the woman who left him for his best friend's brother.

Evidently, they have a ritual that takes everything into account. This evening, at our farewell dinner, we were told that on the first warm day of spring a legend begins circulating among those sitting in the park. It is a great honor to be there, but it is not something one should seek too often. Initially, the legend discussed only the earliest history of the towers. As stories, the priest who received a dream from heaven and the queen who commanded a monument be built in honor of her brave dead husband were used up long ago. Now, our host told us with a smile, the legend must begin elsewhere—not in dreams and memory, but in daylight and desire.

Anyone can add whatever they like to the story, or take some chunk of it away, if, in their opinion, it impedes the narrative flow. At the beginning of summer (or the tourist season) the story, by then refined into its smoothest chapters, is written down by the mayor. A vote is taken by the council. If it passes approval, which it always does after a few minor revisions are made, the story is sealed away in a vault.

In the fall, when school begins, the children of the island are taught the story in their classes. It becomes the basis for the entire curriculum; literature, mathematics, even biology and the other natural sciences. In this way the children learn what must be forgotten, if they are to continue sleeping in their whitewashed cottages by the sea.

The Pleasures of Exile

About an hour before dawn the women squeeze themselves into wicker chairs. Directly before each of them is a window overlooking the town square. All the windows have long since agreed on one thing; there is a fountain overflowing with dried black leaves, and a stray dog snapping at the moonlight.

In just a few minutes the statue in front of the hospital will begin raising his sword ever so slightly, hoping to make the sun appear a moment or two sooner to the bedridden. Later, in the lengthening shadows of the blue afternoon, the sword will be lowered, as if the day had stayed long enough.

It is said that only he, with his medals and faraway gaze, can find the door the sun must take in order to reach the next village. No one has ever bothered to go there, though it is said to lie just beyond the forest.

None of these stories interest the women sitting in front of their windows. They are too busy trying not to be fooled by the wind. From the way they are sitting, from the tilt of their heads, it is clear that they all agree on one thing; they want to hear the approaching footsteps of their husbands and sons, the shifting of loose stones on the gravel path.

When they hear the first sounds to come across the distance, they know their husbands and sons are about to enter the town square, quickly and efficiently. Then each of them will turn without ceremony toward the appropriate street, the correct door.

Finally, when the last man enters the last door, all the curtains are drawn. The engines of the sun are about to arrive. Day will start, while, nearby, the wind will stir in the meadow, a restless dreamer.

A few moments after dawn spills down the mountain, a bird begins carrying pebbles in his beak. Hour after hour, the husbands and sons share in this task of circling a field, finding a pebble, soaring over the bay.

Sometimes, I felt as if my wings were the arms of a man rowing against the tide, my boat piled high with cargo.

Other times, I am a pebble dropped again and again.

I know I shall wake up in the next village and be the shadow of the dog barking at the ribbon of moonlight swirling around and around his legs.

I stop and look up at the windows.

They are listening intently to the wind roaming through the orchards.

The first apple is beginning its descent.

All I know is that years from now, when its glistening torso rolls across these cobblestones, no children will come out to greet it.

Corpse and Mirror I

1

When one of our citizens dies, his corpse is placed in his chariot. To help him reach his destination, his favorite horses are buried with him.

By the time the dawn breaks out of its cage in the mountains, the gravediggers have gently lowered the chariot and its contents into a pit. Now, the horses must be rounded up and measured with the precision of a tailor. For each of these nervous engines must fit smoothly into its own grave, so only the head with its fearful yet fiery eyes emerges above the ground, like a hand rising from the sea.

Once the gravediggers have accomplished this task, they return immediately to the city. Their pace is quickened by the knowledge that inside their kitchens steam has started rising from glistening slabs of meat, tureens of brightly colored vegetables, and baskets of earth-colored breads.

All afternoon they have dreamed of entering a room like this, full of solace and celebration. And yet, when each of them reaches its door, they hesitate, almost as if they wished they could join the procession of heads towing an invisible cargo toward the setting sun, the next city that must be reached before dawn escapes once more.

If the man's sins outweigh his acts of kindness, the horses will eventually collapse and blood will stream from their nostrils. Beneath the moon the man will revive, but he will have become so hideously ugly since his last breath left him that no one—not even the most generous of Samaritans—will be able to offer him food and shelter. He will remain in this condition, doomed to wander in the desert, like a vulture without wings.

The only way he will be given another chance is if one of his neighbors dreams about him in the week following his death. In the dream the man must give his exact location beneath the stars.

At dawn, the neighbor must ride out to the spot and see if he is there. If he isn't, the kindhearted neighbor must dismount at once and begin praying, for he has been deceived once again. Death has not prevented the deceased from continuing along the path he chose in life. If the neighbor does not pray at once, he must give up all hope of ever finding his way back to the city. The dead man has chosen him for a companion, and he has been foolish enough to accept.

2

When one of our citizens dies, his head is cut off and placed inside a mirror-lined box. The box is tightly sealed, allowing no light to enter its interior, and placed inside the least used room of the house. Each night, someone from the family must sleep beside the varnished cube in which the head resides. After two weeks have elapsed, the box can be buried beside the rest of the corpse.

However, if everyone in the family bears a grudge against the deceased, an anger so deep that death has not removed its poison, they may burn the box and joyfully kick the ashes and bone fragments into the river. This decision must be reached without ever being mentioned. Finally, once the ashes begin floating downstream, the deceased's name can never be brought up in conversation again.

Once the head is inside the box, the eyelids will push against the weight of dreams and sleep until they open. It will never occur to him that his head has been severed from his body. Instead, he will believe he has been kidnaped and buried in the sand. Before him is a road stretching to the horizon. Above him the moon patrols the walls of its vast domain. Escape is impossible. By morning the vultures will begin circling patiently.

Soon he begins rambling, imagining his mouth is parched and full of sand. This is a signal. Whoever is sleeping in the room must awaken immediately and begin listening to the voice echoing inside the box. What happens next depends on who has died. If instructions are uttered, they must be followed faithfully. If a confession is made, it must be heard without judgment. Whatever is said must be kept a secret.

If you are sent to another city, you must saddle your horse at dawn and leave without speaking to anyone. Once you are there, you must find the house the voice described. A house similar to all the houses on all the winding streets in this haphazardly designed city, and yet different in one essential way. When the door opens you will know why. However, if the person who answers the door is puzzled by your request, then you have failed to listen to the instructions carefully enough. Too many words slipped through your excitement. In this case, you must return to your house without speaking to anyone along the way. No one in your family will greet you. You cannot sleep beside the box again, but must remain inside your room until the two weeks are over.

One night, after the box has been buried or burned, you will hear something outside your window, inside your dream. The words may not be words at all, but the fluttering of a bird caught in a snare. A broken pot. A bucket falling into a well. Listen carefully. He may need to speak to you once again.

Corpse and Mirror II

1

When a comet passes over the town, whoever sees it knows a corpse will be discovered at the edge of the forest shortly after dawn.

Last week, an old woman, who embroiders tablecloths with human hair, saw one from her kitchen window, and knew her grandson had wandered too far from the road leading home.

Now, whenever she stops to talk to someone, she asks: "Was the message delivered too early? Or remembered too late?"

If they are lying faceup with their eyes open and clear, as if they are still puzzled by the last thing they saw, then they must be cremated, their ashes scattered over the lake.

If, however, they are lying facedown with their eyes closed, as if they had dozed off while recalling the intricate lattice of a pleasant hour they passed through years ago, then they must be buried at once. No stone can mark the spot.

Otherwise, both the deceased and its discoverer are doomed to remember a moment, its sunlit basket of fruit, as if each drop of significance will elude them forever.

Some find it impossible to believe their life is chained to a comet. If they were to submit to the possibility the stars have exiled us from their provinces, then they would have to accept that the story unfolds without them.

In the afternoon, you see them huddled in the corners of dark cafes. Sometimes, their mumbling reaches the street the way the sound of dry branches rubbing against each other pierces a dream.

Then one is awakened by a comet passing overhead; and once again the light echoing in our eyes reminds us that we are meant to wander from one day to the next, like dogs without masters.

2

When you break a mirror, you must count up the pieces to see if they are equal to your age. If they are, you must change your name and leave town at once.

Do not speak to anyone you meet on the road until you have reached a town, where everyone speaks a language different from your own. Otherwise, you will wake up in someone else's coffin.

Do not tell anyone your name until you have forgotten every endearment (affectionate or otherwise) you were summoned by as a child. Otherwise, one morning, the only voice you hear will be your own, echoing down the long hallways beneath sleep.

The voice will begin telling you a story about a child who hears someone calling his name. No matter which way the child turned, the source of the voice eluded him. And, as the story enters daylight's tenement, you will realize that you are the child, and it is your voice calling.

Corpse and Mirror III

1

When the movie ends and the lights come on, the audience is puzzled by the sight of a corpse reclining on a velvet couch in clothes of human hair. Each item has been carefully woven together, so that the hair resembles a white silk shirt and a three-piece wool suit flecked with gold.

On the mahogany table is a brass ashtray in the shape of a bulldog. Smoke curls from its nostrils as if it had swallowed a cigarette. An emerald butterfly glistens on his left index finger. In his bluish gray hands is a book whose pages are made of glass.

The next afternoon I drive to the outskirts of town, where there is a restaurant named after a traitor famous for his ingenious disguises. Many of its patrons think that even the name is a disguise, and that he still moves among us.

I have never been able to remember the plot of the movie, only the colors it traced against the arch of the bridge connecting the room's two halves together. On one side shines the movie and on the other sits the corpse. Passing back and forth between them is a conversation made of human hair.

2

When the movie ends, the lights come on. The audience is puzzled by the sight of a large oval mirror leaning awkwardly against a column, which wasn't there at the beginning of the evening's entertainment.

Scarves stop fluttering; and, one by one, hands settle nervously into laps, like birds circling the parameters of their nests. Mouths twist beneath the receding wave of whispers, almost as if there were a place they could hide.

A reflection pierces the mirror, though the stage is empty. The men see a woman brushing her hair, while the women see a man trimming his beard.

Later, no one will be able to agree on what they saw. The memory of one event will twist around the memory of another. All that remains is the ache of trying to recall a moment, whose slanting roof of sunlight has long since fallen in. By then the mirror will have vanished and the movie will have started. This time in pieces.

Variations on Corpse and Mirror

1

When a corpse meets a corpse there is a mirror between them.

2

Hours before the game is scheduled to start, the arena is packed. Arriving from the east with the necessary backdrop is the sky, speckled with clouds, and carrying a pale yellow sun. Pennants wag their image of a dog with a blue and green tongue. Rows of amulets bob up and down.

3

A few centaurs guffaw and stamp their hooves. Others are content to whisper quietly about the possible combinations. Bets are made between friends and among rivals. Conversations start and end with money, while, here and there, an empty cup (sign of impatience) floats down from the upper tiers, littering an otherwise empty field.

4

Short white hair, turquoise dress. She stands at the bus stop, aware that she has forgotten to bring the flowers. By now, the sun is shuffling its yellow cards beside the note on the counter.

5

In the restaurant surrounded by alligators munching their way through another evening of entertainment. In the next room, someone turns the page and laughs.

6

Sunlight flopped over the windowsills facing the sea.

7

In another room in another house in another city tears are labeled according to consistency and circumstance.

8

She quashes her need to moan, perhaps scream, and chooses instead a soft sigh meant to attract attention without eliciting a response. In the next room, someone shuffles money and laughs.

9

Once, in a month of blue moons, they found lodging in Siena, while people ran through the streets screaming. Feverish with the news or news of the fever?

10

During the night, legions of centaurs had amassed on the hills overlooking the city. By noon, their guns gleamed like teeth, but their teeth still chattered. Matted fur of an army that marched for days in the rain.

11

The smell burns the nostrils for weeks. The piles of hooded and twisted limbs mounting at every streetcorner. They begin staying in their room. They begin talking as if the past is all they have to look forward to.

12

He imagines her in a short white dress, with flowing turquoise hair. They dance beneath the chandelier of stars. Or beneath the bandages a face hidden behind a face.

13

Satisfied everyone could see what they had paid to witness, the architect left the stadium without noticing the clouds circling the sun. Or without cornices, arches, and pillars, bands of masons were able to construct an arena near the center of the city. Vacant eyesocket pierced by centuries of sunlight and rain, the twin javelins elected to guard the city.

14

I left the stadium when the outcome was no longer in doubts. Birds were struggling to form a red necklace above the rooftops. Later, I saw waves leapfrogging in the harbor, stone after stone sliding into place, until a boat tilted precariously among the pyramids of ice.

15

From his seat he watches, hears himself whisper, fear etching its imprint into the tunnel burrowing through his voice.

16

Often she turned, and turned away. Slender neck above a white dress. What she remembered most was the moon's cold and bitter wine.

17

That morning they stood at the bus stop, each wishing the other would mention what had happened to the flowers. Neither of them was able to start the conversation, and on the bus it became impossible to talk, when a group of raucous students stamped their feet, and waved black and yellow pennants.

18

Everything else happened shortly before noon. Shortly before I saw eggshells drifting across the harbor. By then the sounds had started reaching us; and we knew that just outside the city walls someone had nailed a note to the sky, and someone else's forehead was bleeding.

Variations on Corpse and Mirror (Second Set)

I crossed
the street

but not
before

noticing the knife
poised along

the moment's throat,
ready to divide

its destination
into two further choices.

In the yard beside me
dogs played catch

with someone's head
while a hand

waved goodbye
to the body

it once carried

Two Meditations on Guanajuato

(for Clark Rodewald)

1

Postcards are fragments of an encyclopedia; and typical of one announcing a town whose existence concerns only its tenacious inhabitants, this one's a photograph of its rather unique main attraction. San Antonio has its fort, Lugano its lake. But for those stopping in Guanajuato to take in the sights, the main attraction seems to be a little graveyard museum. The treasures lining its walls are some former citizens, all recently deceased. For the photograph, seven mummies have been carefully posed: three adults and four infants.

On the back of the postcard is written: "Well, yes, there are mummies in Guanajuato — They dig you up after five years in the crowded graveyard, but this is wonderful dry climate and preserves bodies — some of them — and the lucky ones get stood up in a hallway of some kind of graveyard museum — there's even a lady died during Caesarean operation and the kid on the umbilical cord with her. But I think the reason they won't decay is that they like their beautiful town so much they can't leave it."

At first glance, they look like neighbors posing for a photograph taken at a suburban Halloween party. The adults have been propped up on a ledge about two feet above the floor. The woman has been placed between the two men. And, unlike her escorts, she has been placed in a wooden coffin, which resembles a doorway to a tiny vestibule and has a pointed arch. It must be sunny and warm outside, for she is wearing what was once a white linen dress. Her arms are casually folded, as she has only stopped by for a moment to tell us what she has just learned about the butcher and his long-nosed wife.

Both her escorts are nearly lost in their ill-fitting three-piece suits. A pocket watch dangles from the vest of the man on the left. Is one of the curator's duties to wind the watch every morning?

The baggy suits and dress reveal one aspect of the geology. If you are buried in the soil of Guanajuato, you shrink. Everything is squeezed out of you, like a sponge, until only the essential elements remain.

The man on the left is clutching his chest with both hands in obvious hysteria. His mouth is agape, his face contorted. Has he just realized he has lost his wallet and cannot pay the bill? Has he only just this minute consulted his watch and seen what time it is? Or was it simply that he was buried alive? And his mouth is permanently open in the belief someday his screams would finally reach us.

The man on the right, shoulders stooped under an invisible weight, appears to be the most uncomfortable of the three. His arms dangle uselessly at his sides and his head is turned slightly toward the woman. He has been paying attention to her for a long time—longer than even he can remember—and knows it is not the same as listening to a cab driver complain about what his wife fixed him for breakfast.

At the bottom of the woman's coffin is a child dressed in red, its head bowed and solemn. Were they buried together? And why?

The other children are dawdling on the floor. If anything, they are a ragged band of devoted cherubs. Like the angels, their sex is unclear, for they are all wearing the same kind of loose-fitting smock one sees in a hospital.

Despite the comic overtones of their narrative, everyone in the postcard radiates a persona of dignified homeliness. This condition is intensified by its irrevocability, as well as by the woman's ceaseless blathering, the man's permanent discomfort, and the realization the bill can never be rendered in full. And yet, for all their endless troubles, they seem genuinely relaxed, now that they are on eternal vacation from the inescapable poverty of Guanajuato.

There is something familiar about the way this collection of corpses is huddled in front of the camera, the way the men are attending to a woman's needs. Their iconographic counterparts can be discovered in Masaccio's panel, *Madonna and Child with Saints*. In the painting everyone is stiff, homely, and graceful. Many scholars believe the deliberate stiffness of the Christ Child's pose foretells the rigidity of his death.

Not only do the bodies in the postcard bear a similar pose to those in Masaccio's panel, but there is also a corresponding stiffness to the way their gestures have affected their clothes, whether they are suits or robes, gowns or dresses. In the postcard the clothes have succumbed to the same *rigor mortis* that invaded its inhabitants. And, as with the painting, an oddly natural light exhales throughout.

Clearly, Masaccio and whoever posed the mummies share an iconography, despite a time lapse of more than five hundred years. The biggest difference is in the moment; the painting depicts an event whose outcome is already known, while the postcard records what happens after the inevitability has occurred.

The idea of being able to dig someone up after five years and place their corpse in a museum is a rather grimly comical notion. Our ideas about death are more pristine. We want it clean, the grounds of the cemetery mowed. We do not want flies buzzing around our heads. And we certainly do not want row after row of gaping leerers around to remind us that they might have had the last laugh. Even the names we give our cemeteries suggest the possibility of peace on earth. And yet, I am fascinated by this postcard; and I know if I ever go to Mexico, I will stop in Guanajuato and pay a visit to the inhabitants of its dusty museum.

2

I do not imagine anyone I know, including myself, would like to see their relatives propped up in the hallway of a local museum. Nor can I imagine many people I know would like to see their mother, sister, or wife associated with the Madonna in this fashion. In fact, that much maligned creature, the tour guide and his memorized spiel, is easier to imagine.

"That one over there is my ugly nephew, but this one is my beautiful, darling cousin." We would stop in the hallway, turn and watch him, as he turned to us and continued lamenting the unfairness of fate to grant her such a short, hard life. Existence had been sucked out of her by the sun and soil itself, until all that remained of her was what we saw before us; a young, wizened girl in tatters.

When we finally reached the exit, he would remind us once again of the holes in her cotton dress, while each of us fumbled for change, knowing he would spend it later that evening in a bar. We might even return the following day to see if he chose another resident or changed his story. But more than likely we would continue our journey through Mexico, knowing whatever he said the second time would not remove the memory of what we first saw.

Isn't my urge to go to Guanajuato similar to the one I have when I go to the bookstore and buy an autobiography or biography? I want to know something more about someone. It is the only reason I look at photographs; Guanajuato's museum, for example. So why do I read autobiographies if I am unwilling to write one? It grows more complicated. For the postcard has become increasingly entangled with the idea of Christmas, my memories of it. And if the connection has remained constant yet vague—which it has—comical yet dull and unspecified, like a restless ache, then I must make it clear, at least to myself, if I am to get on with my daily activities.

In fact, I no longer need the postcard to prompt my memory. For months I have seen their wrinkled faces peering out of everyone I know. Their taut smiles, barely controlled hysteria, and relentless discomfort debut when least expected.

I am unable to think of Christmas without remembering Guanajuato. They are like Siamese twins, one unable to breathe without the other. I know I must understand why they seem permanently joined. Otherwise, I am stuck, forever repeating their images in my mind, seeing their contorted faces while listening to a friend convey an anecdote.

Nothing seems to remove this distraction. And yet, if I am going to dig up the recent past and place it in a museum, if I am going to endow its banality with meaning, as anyone who writes about themselves does, I want it done quickly and efficiently, like the men who push their spades into the warm soil of Guanajuato. For it will be a museum I have no desire to visit. Arranging it will be enough.

Carp and Goldfish

1

Some fish we peel back, leaving only the bones. Others devour us, leaving only the stories. This one begins in a garden in China, where a young prince is sitting alone on a bench beside a turquoise pond. Each time he snaps his fingers and whistles, the golden red sunset of a carp can be seen rising toward the surface.

Five fat scavengers rule this delicately manicured kingdom, and each of them has been endowed with the nobility of a name. When the boy leaves the palace at noon and walks across the garden to feed them, the moment is as precise and refined as the emblematic flowers stitched over his robe.

On a warm summer afternoon the pond is as green as nights in the Arctic when embedded arrows of light sparkle in the sky.

For a few moments the boy watches the clouds stretch across the glassy surface. Soon it will be his sixth birthday, and another carp will join the kingdom.

The clouds turn into dragons and back again. The moon trembles against the sky, a slivered almond. One day melts into another.

In the pond the carp are still listening, unable to hear their names drift over the kingdom. The prince is sick and they have been forgotten. Patiently, they circle through their palace, looking for the entrance to the room where their master lies, his body burning with fever, his face as crimson as an apple, ripe and ready to fall. Above them only the murmur of the wind hurrying through the mulberry branches.

Eventually, the countryside succumbs to disease and terror. Succeeding reigns of tyrants — their names twisting through history like snakes — bury the pond beneath their own interpretation of heaven's grandeur. Meanwhile, the carp burrow into a book written by someone whose ability to remember facts circumscribes his desire to tell stories.

2

To the young boy standing in front of the large glass tanks, each hypnotic with activity, all the goldfish looked more or less the same. It was only after he stared into one tank for a long time that he saw any difference among them. He chose the two smallest, the ones that would have the most trouble surviving were someone to let them go.

When he got home, his father lay on the couch and took a nap. His mother was out visiting a friend. Already the shadows of the narrow street had started filing quietly into the room.

He lay on his stomach on the floor and stared intently at the fish. Back and forth they swam, unconcerned with their intruder. They looked as if the only thought on their minds was escape. It was difficult to name creatures so alien and indifferent, and he had not been able to find any that he liked.

As the fish darted from side to side, the young boy wondered what he could do to make them more comfortable. They must get tired, he thought. And yet, they do not seem sleepy. The room was filled with the signs of evening's approach. He lay in the darkness and remembered the way the ocean rocked endlessly the day his parents took him to the beach. Beside him the fish swirled once more in their bowl. Nearby, his father snored.

In the bedroom he found his dump truck beside a pile of soldiers and blocks, and brought it back into the living room. Carefully, so as to not spill any water, he placed the fishbowl on the back of the truck. Then he lay on the floor and began slowly pushing the truck back and forth. His father stirred slightly and then sank back into sleep.

The boy watched the water sloshing against the sides of the bowl, like the ocean, and was momentarily relieved. He adjusted the speed with which he moved the truck to a slower, more rhythmic pace.

Then he realized what they needed besides this comforting motion was salt. He remembered the stinging taste of the waves as they tried to knock him over, his mother beside him so he would not be afraid.

One teaspoon, a little more rocking, and they soon would be asleep. His arm was tired, but he continued to push the truck back and forth in the darkened room. He knew he could not stop until they were resting, comfortable in their new home.

CHILDHOOD
(1984)

Cenotaph

I

The clues to what they remembered had been pasted into an album. Photographs of her family and friends, snapshots he had taken during the war. The album was packed neatly in a trunk, which was then stored in the ship's hold. It was nearly spring when they sailed from Shanghai to San Francisco.

II

The album was not, as the word suggests, white. Its pages were black — the time inside the camera before light casts its shadows on the wall. What were white were the words, the laconic summations printed along the bottom of every page.

III

The album was divided into two parts, his and hers. In the second part, his part, someone (most likely her) had carefully removed the snapshots. It was here I always slowed down and inspected the pages. The place where the words were lined up beneath black rectangles.

IV

What had reflected the light was gone. Only the rows of white letters remained. Only the faded rectangles framing empty black spaces.

V

I would spin in my room until I was too dizzy to stand. Then, lying on the bed with my eyes closed, I would pretend the plane was about to crash.

VI

Those black rectangles surrounded by faded black almost blue frames. The words were arranged neatly along the bottom of every page. My father was an accountant, this was his ledger.

VII

I understood someone had tried to erase this history of excerpts. The words continued echoing long after I returned the album to its place on the shelf.

VIII

The hospital was next to the jail. From the roof I could see the inmates playing basketball, the interns practicing their serves.

IX

I tried imagining the pictures the black rectangles once held. *Mound of Heads, Shanghai, 1946* was my favorite. Movies showed me everything but this.

X

At the beach I saw the words transformed by the sun. Saw them become hills of bleached skulls. Now they were smooth and round, white as the words describing them.

XI

Lying beside the sagging castles, watching the sand trickle through my fingers. Tiny examples of what I read. All afternoon I played beneath the sun with the skulls, molding them into little mountains.

Cenotaph of Snow

I

Snow is both durable and deceiving. It can be shaped into a wall or squeezed into a weapon.

II

One night, during a storm, they use it to erase every sign of their entry into a village. Lying down in rows beside the white wooden church, sinking beneath the snow, waiting for dawn to thaw the sky.

III

Soft glistening field, treacherous blanket.

IV

Shortly before dawn the sexton and his two oldest sons begin clearing the steps and making paths. A few neighbors pitch in. Thin ropes of smoke start curling from the chimneys. Birds, sunlight, bells, then prayer.

V

The bells united the villagers kneeling inside the church with the men waiting beneath the snow. They located precisely where in the narrative everyone could be found.

VI

After his father reads him the story, he begins each night by pulling the blanket over his head and listening. Will he be able to stay awake long enough to hear the bells? Has he finally learned how to shape his dreams? Afraid of the answer, he retells the story once more.

VII

It was during moments like these—ones of calm frenzy—that he wished he could become like the bells, and float above the consuming flames. Surely, the more he repeated the story, the more likely he would hear them echoing in the dome enclosing his head.

VIII

The closer he got to sleep, the harder it was to discover if he was kneeling inside the church or hiding beneath the snow. In order to keep circling, he had to tell himself the story once more.

IX

Even now, years later, a cold soft pillow greets his falling head.

Halfway to China

I

While lying on a beach, he remembers the photographs he once saw in a magazine. On a strip of white sand, nestled between the movie lot palm trees and sculpted turquoise waves. Beneath the brownish-red mask that clamps tightly over his face when he closes his eyes.

The children—their eyes are open and their faces immobile.

II

Later in the afternoon, images of the children return while he is crossing a bridge that arcs its dinosaur spine between two islands off the coast of Florida.

III

The fish are shiny envelopes full of old news. Slit open, cracked through—seagulls wait their turn. Pink and silver flashes piled on broad wooden planks. Songs, gossip, shrill squawks, bartering.

IV

On the boardwalk, the heads and shells of turtles are sold from carts. Lined up according to size, like shoes. Emptying in order to fill. The dried and hardening layers of skin. The body is an accessory— something no longer needed to propel it from place to place.

V

At the end of the holidays, the student took one back to college and placed it on a shelf overlooking his cluttered room.

The first few times she stuck her tongue out at it, just as he was about to have orgasm. Then, one afternoon, she laughed. She couldn't help it, she told her friends, because it seemed as if it were winking at her.

Gargoyle—throat, gullet.

VI

Christopher Columbus thought the islands were off the coast of India. Ponce de Leon stopped here to pick up supplies. Florida—the "feast of flowers"—swallows him up. And Henry Hudson and his sons were set adrift by the mutinous crew of his ship, *Discovery*. In the New World, they were dinosaurs. We are left with names: the capital of landlocked Ohio; a penis-shaped state inhabited by bathrobes and crocodiles; a dirty river used for dumping unwanted bodies.

VII

But today, on a beach near a golf course and a riding academy, it is the world that is stationary. And you are floating above it, miles away from your nearest neighbor.

VIII

Incas guided groups of children up the mountain, and left them as offerings to their gods. They have been waiting for centuries when they are discovered by accident. Frozen and intact. Replicas of themselves. Ice, not wax. Brightly woven blankets their crustacean shells.

IX

Narcotics convinced them they were invincible. Just as they helped young kidnaped boys believe they had died and entered the Valley of Paradise.

Thug canoe barbecue hashish dungarees assassin tomahawk — words absorbed from cultures designated as Indian.

X

Shanghai — to drug and kidnap for service as a sailor.

XI

The first time he saw someone imprisoned by ice was when he was a child sitting alone in a movie theater.

XII

A bearded man squats outside a cave, a rifle cradled in his arms. Inside, a younger man shivers, his gun empty. The rest of the movie is a slow-motion dance between a lizard and a butterfly.

XIII

The curtains of snow are parted by a pale yellow sun. Still dazed by the storm, a herd of buffalo wanders past the bearded man, who sits motionless in front of a pile of ashes. A close-up of his tense face and unblinking eyes. Snow clings to his beard.

XIV

The last scene is always the first to be remembered. The butterfly kicks the lizard and watches him topple over. Wax, not ice.

XV

Other movies, actors, and stories. But this one never starts and the men have no names.

XVI

Images swirl through the afternoon. Clouds cast blue shadows. Hair turning to strings of ice, a statue lying on its side. Ants slide down slopes and forage in craters. Two voices discuss the weather as if it has stopped on another, nearby island.

XVII

The children were arranged in rows.
A silent society, a secret one.

XVIII

Beneath the mask he remembers his friend telling him a story about what it was like to grow up in China. After being led into the room, she was ordered to go over to the canopied bed, draw the curtain back, and kiss her dead grandmother farewell.

We Are All Vultures

The man in the next bed died just after eating lunch. You were staring at his daughter, and wondering what she looked like in a silver nightgown. She had just finished telling you about a dream she had had the night before: You had fallen out of bed, but the traction pin held you upside down, as if you were an animal waiting to be slaughtered. She was running to save you, but kept tripping over her nightgown.

Of course, the dream was about her father and not you. Still, you were staring at her and wondering if you would ask the obvious: Why didn't you take off your nightgown.

You didn't. She would have been embarrassed about taking off her clothes in front of strangers. And you were equally uneasy about asking her why she didn't.

That was twelve years ago, and you never saw her again.

The nurses drew the curtain, wheeled him out, emptied his locker, and sponged down the mattress. All you could do was listen.

What is terrible (and beautiful) about the past is its remoteness. There are things that happen to you long before you are born. Sometimes, they are smoothly in place when your moment comes around.

Somebody leaves. Whatever is left behind will soon be gone, devoured by words.

DRAGON'S BLOOD
(1985–1988)

Cascade

We were sitting outside
the factory of last resorts
drinking tea and talking
around the carved feather,
tumbling into your bagged body
its quivering spokes
baboon brilliant
in the faded spray

It was copper twilight
hushed tunnel when one
good tremble deserves a star

I wish the robots zipping us
into the lower forehead's mirror
burned away the banjo players
their useless hands

I wish their slender vapors
had lodged in our discolored necks
easing the thicket of clamps
I wish I had never seen

the photographs of the women
with no hair, children assembled
in front of the fountain,
grackles and gold teeth

Another wrinkled citizen
I have come to tell you
the sadness machine
is on the fritz again

Seance Music

(for Trevor Winkfield)

Salt starts falling from my tongue
Will the poem arrive soon
How will I recognize it

By the pages flying up from the brain
says the striped man on television
holding an audible tone in his hand

By its radiant crystal apparatus
transmitting harmonic interferences
through the moth-eaten glove of a doll

Salt continued falling from his tongue
as I strolled along the outer aspects of myself
planting passionate incidentals in the mud

Someone's voice had been trapped inside a jar
and yes
the painting of the poem will arrive soon

and the man with the hamburger bun on his head
and the knight in rusty armor swinging a mop
and the chicken who doesn't need his head to sing

and yes
the man in the prison uniform
will leave his imprint in the air

All This Changing Trouble Luck and Suddenness
(after Sidney Bechet)

Some of what came and some were poor
Some could make it up some sat down
Some to hear someone who was playing
I'm glad to be told I started out
I was little and awful and then I was music
Hearing itself above the ceiling
Someone who was playing some to dance
I lengthened the comfort of moving on
Someone to stand with for a distance
Instead of listening to the noise of a clock falling
A string of fish to all that rhythm
Some I made myself out of my remembering

Confessions

She spends her money in the desert, at the movies,
on statues for the lawn

Someone smears her back and thighs with lotion
The latest rage, the newest anger

I have abandoned, kidnaped, or murdered three words
and have no plans to restore them

They enter the funeral home and steal
what they think is their father's body

Someone else squeezed it from a drowned sailor's tongue
Hair shirt, leather pants

I am Napoleon and this Indian is my guide
The road ahead of us speaks the alphabet of fire

Paradise

The motorcycle was saved when the driver's head
was etched by lightning

She spends a weekend on a beach in Crete
without opening her eyes

They kiss as if tomorrow is an island
trickling into the sea

Recoil

Clouds drape moon in striped appeals
We erase the words surrounding us and kiss

under the concrete bridge connecting
last year's popular versions of heaven and hell

Our heads are billboards posted above desire
In each insect welded tunnel

someone enters a chamber of delirium

The Charred Voice of Max Ernst

I too volunteered to monitor
this parched quadrant of infinity,
but that doesn't mean I have to swallow
each drop that is shuttled across

Who says the barriers can be thawed?
Who can prove the vapors will erase themselves?
I've been hearing promises like that
since the moment you started ripping me in two

You Must Remember

not to mumble
not to mangle
the words

you are holding
in your hands
in your head

You must remember
to deliver your head
to the auditorium

where it will be mounted
along with the others
your hands and head

going together
to the auditorium
where someone

maybe more than one
is waiting for you
to deliver your voice

mangled as
it was
formed

You must remember
to return bread
to plate

lift head
from page
You must remember

to chew
before swallowing
to swallow

what's on
plate or page
in your life or hands

You must remember
to deliver the words
mounted on the page

your head
sitting on
the plate

You must remember
these things
as things

that once kept you
from speaking from
a book or box

Red Fountain

When the last mirage
evaporates, I will be
the sole proprietor of this voice
and all its rusted machinery.
I have reread the instructions.
I have hidden the limelight vapors
and flowers of memory.
By tomorrow or the day after,
I will have collected enough
gasoline and lightning.
Do you remember the lipstick imprint?
Is it true he has my name
stamped on his identity card?
The leaves are whiter this year
and another boat has capsized on the lake.
Did I tell you I delivered the letter?
Your eyes are green sometimes blue or brown.
I have mowed the lawn and fed the chickens.
The wind is spinning, but air has settled into the locks.

Medusa

Finally, the remaining distinctions begin
pulling off the wings surrounding sleep.
Another row of gnarled husks is dropped
into the car's illuminated ashtray.
Not even a voice wafer is heard
among the stars' splintered echoes.
Hidden camera freezes her coastline shadow
in neon blaze. No one snickers.
After removing the terrain of her long socks,
unbuckling steel garlands, notched hitch,
and safety belt, she enters the newly painted dome.
Will she believe the legend wilting on mirror's pond?
When the time comes, will she swallow
her last lizard attention capsule?
I remember the emerald butterfly
pinned to her black nylons.
It was snowing behind the barn.
As long as the anchorites remain suspended
from yesterday's dust cloud, I can hide
among the squadrons of their dying flares.
I've been gobbled by slick eon worms
while tracking Abe Snake, glared mindlessly
at battered instrument panels, memorized
tell-tale fibers, pixel by pixel.
Who started handing out lifetime guarantees?
She knows a man painted with four rotating legs
creates the illusion of walking. What good
to hide the motor in a suitcase?
You must always wear borrowed clothes,

know in which elevator you can lease
the best advice, grind cashews with steel.
Armed monkeys make the best companions.
Remember the different ways water splashes
across scissors, convertibles, and apricots.
Another trick you must keep up the sleeve
beneath your tongue, the lace twilight between them.
Trumpet strands unravel above parking lot
circling wishing well's medicine chest.
Adamant grins, comfortable grimaces.
A tourist among hibiscus, a bus driver
clearing the table of beetles.
Under the circumstances
a larger tray of gestures
is no longer permitted
to be carried from the plantation garden.
Why's she smiling at her watch?
Why's her sister counting the hands
sweeping through her hair?
We were ordered to rent a body
and carry it to the post office.
We had to wait until the right moment
but it never arrived. Do you remember
the time I kissed you, full and hard,
in front of your husband?
You had shown me a postcard—
rustling heaps inside a hive
meant for children. Shadows
sliced the room in half.
Yes, I too became what you predicted.

Return of Ulysses I

They do not believe they visited islands that never existed. One morning, they are sawed in half. Dream after dream, like buckets of wet black mud dumped on our heads. I will tell a different story each time I am asked. On the inside of her thigh, in a ring of pink stars, is tattooed the dead actor's thumbprint, her dressmaker's initials, and a lost air micro-chip leased by a bank in Panama. My name is in the glove compartment of a Ford Galaxy, on the masthead of the Wild and Sultry Clarion, and in the guest book of the Hotel of Last Regrets. I will visit you when a horse prances across the sky, its cloud a blue rectangle, a window facing the sea, an empty verandah, leaves choking the gutters. I will say nothing. I will point to where the words have been erased from the blackboard, instead.

Return of Ulysses II

We were walking from one end of the island to the other. She told me a story, and showed me a mirror or lie. Behind the wall of reason grazes the lunar horse, she said, as she led me to a window overlooking a courtyard. Thirty men shoveled sand onto the dark blue cobblestones. Inside the stable, teams of actors dyed their bodies the same color as their uniforms. A member of the "green" team practiced sticking his head into the mouth of a lion. He was a penniless duke with a penchant for chocolate. In her story I am followed by a spear of lightning, and its mirror of lies. I escape to another island, where I meet an old woman who describes everything I have ever seen. One morning a torso emerges from the sea.

Why Did What Was When

1

At first the game had rules, but in recent centuries they were replaced by referees. Nine gentlemen wear striped silk shirts (the patina of fireflies against a dying sun) and carry a box turtle tucked neatly under their right arm. If after they've had a conference they still cannot reach a decision, the head referee (the one with the blue and gold eagle tattooed on his right eye) marches to the chalk pentagram in the center of the arena, and begins rhythmically shaking the turtle. Everyone is quiet, almost breathless, waiting for it to yield an answer that can be interpreted in one of three ways. Vultures circle overhead, knowing they are expected to attend the victory party. Blue feathers fall from the upper rungs of the sky.

2

At first the game had rules, but now the arena is a swamp from which we emerge, dragging our victims across the sand. I take the first exit pointing north, and begin counting pink shoes on yellow soil, runny eyes, toothless maws, and parks named after heroines who were either poisoned or burned. The outline of the city returns days after I pass through its empty precincts, a headless statue glowing on every lawn. *Above the gates is carved a story that cannot be repeated without the mistakes becoming a part of the telling.*

Engines of Gloom and Affection

The sky is green, and there is no book to tell us what it means. It has never stopped raining. Three men, four of them speaking. A woman carries a photograph of worms under her tongue. I have spoken out of turn. The proportions are awkward, the details coarse.

The sky is green, and there is no book to tell us the names of our children. Have you noticed the dead man hugging a doll? Have you thought about why she found it necessary to laugh so loudly? And why, for example, the heads of the statues were removed and stored in a vault beneath the hospital?

The sky is green, and there is no book to show us the route. Once a week, he forgets where he parked his car and must return to his apartment. A set of instructions has been placed on the kitchen table. Since his breathing apparatus is so poorly developed, he is confined to driving beside the wall of stucco clouds circling the plaza. The sky is gray mixed with green. Someone claims to be your friend.

Dream Report

You learn the names of trees
for sale on an island

whose owner walks
bareheaded in the rain

eroded by rumors of a life
spent immersing himself

his wife and children
in the rust of human kindness

Dragon's Blood I

I know all dreams grow to the size of a grapefruit
The highway circles the mountain of red mirrors
I check the map and count the stones
As the train chugs past the painting of your face

The highway circles the mountain of red mirrors
Shimmering beneath my eyelids
As the train chugs past the painting of your face
Butterflies hang upside down in winter

Shimmering beneath my eyelids
Is a procession of men on donkeys
Butterflies hang upside down in winter
On the picnic grounds named after your muddy sighs

Is a procession of men on donkeys
A symbol or an indecipherable ribbon
On the picnic grounds named after your muddy sighs
I've buried my blue and yellow paintbrushes

A symbol or an indecipherable ribbon
I check the map and count the stones
I've buried my blue and yellow paintbrushes
I know all dreams grow to the size of a grapefruit

Dragon's Blood II

I recheck the map and count the stones
On the battlefield's neoclassical plain
Someone's ransacked the archives of description
But the statue knows its electrons are aimed at his body

On the battlefield's neoclassical plain
Men dig for vowels and consonants
But the statue knows its electrons are aimed at his body
Like detectives circling a meteor's imprint

Men dig for vowels and consonants
Looking for the missing words dipped in ink
Like detectives circling a meteor's imprint
They must find what has never arrived

Looking for the missing words dipped in ink
Something poets do, muttered grumpy Plato
They must find what has never arrived
While I try to build a path leading to its absence

Something poets do, muttered grumpy Plato
Someone's ransacked the archives of description
While I try to build a path leading to its absence
I recheck the map and count the stones

Dragon's Blood III

As the highway circles the mountain of red mirrors
How did I get stalled above the ribbon of this instance
A woman harvesting opium
In order to sever the transmission filaments

How did I get stalled above the ribbon of this instance
A pebble wrapped in silk
In order to sever the transmission filaments
When I want to parachute into the well

A pebble wrapped in silk
Do I embroider speechlessness
When I want to parachute into the well
Shimmering beneath your eyelids

Do I embroider speechlessness
While you scatter the rainbow of ink
Shimmering beneath your eyelids
Must I now drink milky tears

While you scatter the rainbow of ink
A woman harvesting opium
Must I now drink milky tears
As the highway circles the mountain of red mirrors

Dragon's Blood IV

As the train chugs past the painting of your face
Slats of moonlight enthralled and entwined
Tonight, I am a tuft of blue shadow
Framed by a doorway, watching us dance

Slats of moonlight enthralled and entwined
Flare unclasped keeps spinning its astral rhapsody
Framed by a doorway, watching us dance
Held in air by air

Flare unclasped keeps spinning its astral rhapsody
O bicycle of lightning, do not dissolve
Held in air by air
I circle the hours we were alive

O bicycle of lightning, do not dissolve
In a well where wishes are made and lost
I circle the hours we were alive
Locked in a story empty of words

In a well where wishes are made and lost
Tonight, I am a tuft of blue shadow
Locked in a story empty of words
As the train chugs past the painting of your face

Choral Amphisbaena

I am learning to see
with my other brain

On the shelves closest to the cloud stations
meteors spiral into cool autumn ponds

Sapphire wisps rise from blue membranes
while radium seeps out of the stalks

I am the younger sister
you never noticed

until rain washed away
the last traces of lipstick

He spent the morning ripping out
the pages of an illustrated novel

and replacing each word
with one consuming less letters

Last night, I wore cotton,
pearl, alligator, and plastic

Shortly after the waiter
brought our appetizers

a band of apivorous crones
began roaming through the park

I am the pimply boy
who delivers pizza to burning houses

They parked their motorcycles in a circle
and filed into the courtyard

Somewhere someone
was boiling shoes

I am the silky rodent
who pulls the carriage

from one end of the sentence
to the other

I have been told I look happy
for brief periods

most often when passing
a snow covered golf course

No One Ever Tried To Kiss Anna May Wong

She's trying to find a way to turn her cup
upside down, while sequestered on a train
from Dublin to Vienna. Every angle
glistens from behind a celluloid scrim.
She's wearing a crescent scarf
and chilly snake high smile:
others claim she's all skin and eyes.
No longer lashed to this oily chatter
I enter her compartment.

                              She's languishing
on a ledge, annoyed at all the times
she's been told to be scratched, kicked,
slapped, bitten, stabbed, poisoned, and shot.
Lightning flickers between the frames.
On the seat beside me I find a circle
smaller than one left by a wet apple.

Sam Spade Haiku

Perfect oval
Unlaced leather smile
Tall drink of water
Fist full of trouble

Dark intermissions
Satin waist nipper
Coal blue lips
Pink alabaster burden

Genghis Chan: Private Eye I

I was floating through a cross section
with my dusty wine glass, when she entered,
a shivering bundle of shredded starlight.
You don't need words to tell a story,
a gesture will do. These days,
we're all parasites looking for a body
to cling to. I'm nothing more
than riffraff splendor drifting past the runway.
I always keep a supply of lamprey lipstick around,
just in case.
                She laughed,
a slashed melody of small shrugs.
It had been raining in her left eye.
She began: a cloud or story
broken in two maybe four places,
wooden eyelids, and a scarf of human hair.
She paused: I offer you dervish bleakness
and glistening sediment.
                              It was late
and we were getting jammed in deep.
I was on the other side, staring at
the snow covered moon pasted above the park.
A foul lump started making promises in my voice.

Genghis Chan: Private Eye II

I looked down,
more slender
than I expected

                She was
wearing white under white
gray blond curls dropped back
turned into a block

Across the room, a mirror
had been drained from the top

Clouds buzzed above burgeoning trees
their neat brochures

Their apartment had been flung open
ceiling nibbled at the corners

They had lasted longer than we calculated
refusing to hang up the other's ashes

An ignorant sponge, I had been summoned
to the gate of no mistakes

In less than half a pedal of time
I would be entering the hyena zone

Genghis Chan: Private Eye III

We surfed out of the alley,
the stories our parents told us
trailing behind, like angry yellow toads

You spoke first:
One of my ancestral coupons
composed the bulldozer anthem
Perhaps she too was waiting
for the bumper crop showers
to subside, another dust mote picker
in a long line of lovelorn imports
Yes, I too was stymied by the animal of music
and the shadow its breath sent through history

I wanted to tell you
about the bank teller and the giant,
the red moths hovering above their heads

I wanted to tell you
about the gizmo pit and kinds of sludge
I have cataloged during my investigation

I wanted to tell you
about how the sun
dissolved all of this long ago

leaving us in different rooms

registered under different names

Genghis Chan: Private Eye IV

Rusted pundit, throttled chin

I was turned by a tendril adrift,
pale freckled skin bathed
in insect iridescence,
lips sucked through a straw

Tonight's sampler stops
beside the dialed states,
showroom padlocks coiled
around the vantage points,
gasps clogged in the spray

She was a farm of concrete
cleanly poured, and I
— the quarantined flash —
was tilting above Newt Falls,
its glossy stanzas of imitation snow

Hours of sigh practice loomed ahead

Genghis Chan: Private Eye V

You looked up and said
I spiraled above a forest of necktie splendor
A wooden trembler
hovering above the jetlag lanes
a lost shrieker, I hesitated

You looked up and said
A glass frog with green bones and one red vein
The streets are a lizard in profile
We have strayed from the beehive slag

You looked up and said

Written rewritten blue dust

falls through the cracks

Genghis Chan: Private Eye VI

I am just another particle cloud gliding across the screen

a swamp chanter doodling on the margins of the abyss

I prefer rat back flames to diplomatic curls

I am the owner of one pockmarked tongue

I park it on the hedge between sure bets and bad business

Genghis Chan: Private Eye VII

You will remember the tourist's jawbone
and the end of the erotic age

You will remember how to number
the customized stones of Spartan psychoanalysis

You will be nice to yourself and regret it
You will undress in front of a window overlooking a prison

You will speak to the driver of a blue horse
You will grasp someone's tongue with your teeth and pull

You will prefer the one that bleeds on the carpet
to the one that drools on your sleeve

Texas Sprawl

1

Another barrel of insect casings
spills down the corrugated slants.
This city, he thinks, is frayed
convenience. Its couch is branded
on forehead memorial deposits
locked inside television towers.
Another decade's ooze rides to the top.

2

Her lips are on a stiff diet.
He will have to split his signals elsewhere.
Another transmitter extends her voice
toward the bonfire outlets,
its catalog of endangered critters.
A lard haze shudders inside the crevices.

3

He sits in a refugee car
molting from hum to snarl.
Synthetic apartment appetites.
Horoscopes and hands to hold down
the celebrated intakes of calibrated mist.
Sleek tuxedo sunglasses wrap nylons
in a mountain of spoiled tar.

La Brea

Dozens of blue relics slip from their envelopes, rise and turn toward the sooty pink graveyard of solar automatons. Slate Sunday evening. Deserted malls. Tar bubbling in the fissures spreading beneath her brain.

The refurbished lizard motif, its slanting rows of amber cadaverous eyes, begins blinking above the parking garage. His skin a decrepit compendium to the words he copies down. Egyptian birds and Indonesian bandanas. Ice cream trucks melting in the first dusty moment, its faded tablecloth.

The wind lifted the hats from the rows of dead geniuses, their cold wax frames, and stored them on the upper shelves. I keep a candle near your face, so I might memorize the closet in which you are standing alone. A cab crashes into a tree growing down from the sky, its powdery limits.

A day an apple keeps the doctor away, its doors closed to the fires. Shaped clay twisting in the sparks of water drifting off the screen. Three turtles mingle in the gray azaleas. Some mechanical problems fly ahead.

Cobalt dissipated layers. Birds nest in the trunks of unidentified cars. How to dissect this alternate anatomy, its wet skeleton writhing in the streets?

Another fountain of farm clouds dances on knives and stalks, velvet hunger laughing back.

They painted lips on the back of their hands, while watching guidebooks smoldering in barrels. Someone crossed out the physics of her head. Twilight camera residue injected into thick oblong occurrences.

A thorn of animals discusses the pains they have had to endure.

After placing the money on her tongue, he untied his shoes. The one with the pension and the one with the broken arm.

Manhattan Miniature

The predators removed their harnesses, and vanished into the exposed wires slammed beneath the door. A dwindling oil supply, evaporated ink's milky residue. I was fussing over fragments, and discovering further proofs that I was still snared in the oncoming headlights of a dull mind. They were foolish to look for refuge here. All the rooms of my brain are occupied by dessicated tufts.

Knives surround the cloud shifting inside the leopard skin, its carriage drawn by rows of miniaturized shoes. The figure hunched over the console stops to look once more at the woman curved on the couch. We are their listless pronouns. We live on one of the many aisles advertising the kinds of holdups still available.

The camera tilts back its flow.
The ink reaches its destination.

He returns to the illuminated page of angels hovering above the entrails of a glass city. Too late to rate its action decibels. The insect blood trickling from their lungs has splashed onto the leaves of your empty sequin dress, staining the lace trimmed satin insets and pearl detailing.

Close the book.
Ignore the story.
Write on ropes of twisting smoke.

Spin, Spell, Spill

We met in a crowded auditorium, agreed to rendezvous on a train. Windows on both shelves divided the night into a library. We exchanged the various volumes that remained unwritten, and watched the heat flares seek out the soft side of the stars.

I lift the velvet tourniquet closer to the whale lamp and review the fabled grains, their yellowing history murmuring behind my salvaged eyes. The sky is not quite the color of dawn. It is January, and you are in Bozeman, Montana. I thought I would begin this while you were in the air, above the floor plan of the clouds, their exhumed disarray and brittle gleam.

I have glued the fires together along the thrusts of their throats, fed and washed Mr. and Mrs. Rodent, lolled among the rallying throngs of sawdust noggins, and measured the girth of prize winning museums. Meanwhile, winter shows every sign of extending into a blur. There are no plausible alternatives to the tambourine. I must soon decide if I am going to follow in the footsteps of my jolly neighbors and saunter back into the garage, whistling a tune or humming a melody.

Before writing this, I move the typewriter to the table where we sit in the evening, scraping aromatic scraps off our platters. Delicate rust red lines reproduce a woodland scene presumed to be common to the stories preceding electricity. Two men help each other chop down trees. A woman and a child sit on a log and watch. The wagon is almost full. When we eat dinner, the decaying seepage of this moment is where we stop, our mouths empty.

I spent the night watching the children carry the birds nesting in the volcano down to the skating rink, remembering you drifting above me. In every hollow shadow of fur, I looked for your shoulders, flowing and then applied.

Picture Book

1

The film is gray and wobbly, and shot through with jolts of tarnished light. The unceasing rows of men rise and stumble, twist and flop over, as if someone molded them out of a batter of paste and pebbles. They appear to be rubbery stalks swaying on a distant planet's arid surface. The film doesn't describe what the camera operator was looking at: it remembers a child's jeweled dream, the flickering of eyelids just before dawn. A voice whispers: Some morning, the moon will hide my face.

2

The car has been assembled from pressed tin sheets. It came in a box made of thin gray cardboard that has been folded over and stapled together. The illustration shows an orange and white sedan with a yellow plastic dragon as a hood ornament. The tin sheets have been spray painted white and red. Its silvery tin ornament is a triangular bird-like shape. Three languages describe the box's contents. Both car and box were designed and produced in a country where the bicycle is the most widely used form of transportation.

Predella

I

After removing the anodized plate, the two electricians discover an oblong section of sky behind a row of blue profiles. Dust flows from the holes in his feet. Wires splice them together.

Noon's lush pestilence percolates in the eaves

II

A box mountain of hardened tears is hoisted up the scaffold, two red handkerchiefs securing the throttle. I'm an ignorant cloud smelter. I've come to examine the soot drifting down from empty balconies. When there was no you among many, there were multitudes. Can you tell me where I can find the letters lost from your name?

Tomorrow, at noon, a centaur will be exhibited in the piazza.

III

Beneath sky's broken tiles, ancient barns are embedded in plaster background. A man with a speckled pig arrives by train, under awning of darkness. I enter the postcard districts, where men with pickaxes and coal faces strangle the glow.

Buttons of smudge halt the erosion.

IV

I learn to count without pointing at my fingers. This is Pinocchio, I say. His head's full of sawdust and nails. This is a sordellina, and this the animal from which it was separated.

My feet are twisted.

V

The blessed flagellants set forth, mounted on tatters of flaming horses. Pink mountain path. Loudspeakers at the corners.

I was reading about a man's journey to hell when the phone rang.

VI

She descends the stairway of the last ditch beyond the horizon. I cling to the polished dome enclosing the world. A straw basket or cage hangs outside the shuttered window.

Earrings of blood suspended above the dusty floor.

VII

A charred hansom is discovered on Bubbling Well Road. In the shade of an olive grove two pickpockets argue over their meager hoard. As the last clouds are nailed into place, she watches a scholar from the Eristic School enter the onyx hall.

The heat surrounds us with its necklace of dead birds.

A Suite of Imitations Written After Reading Translations of Poems by Li He and Li Shang-yin

1

When she left she took everything — her hair
Was a dream filled with colors gone by noon.
Yet, if nothing can be retrieved, I am still pulled
Toward this woman, who is still asleep, locked
Away in another life; her hair
Piled up like red peonies at noon.

2

No trace of you in the dust.
No footprints leading away from the house.
All morning I have been walking in this house,
For I am like a pile of dust
Shifting restlessly from room to room.
If you had been a shadow passing through my house,
You would have left nothing behind, not even dust.

3

The clouds change, but my dreams
Of you are always the same.
I see you walking and I call out —
Is it true? I ask, that if you
Dream of your lover, you
Can be assured he has deceived you.
And always, your answer is the same.

How can I tell you? if the only place
We can meet, now, is in these dreams.

4

Your perfume still clings to the dust of this house
If only you had been a ghost and kept your name

If only you had been like the clouds
And drifted over this house

If only I wasn't a foolish old man
Talking to the shadows gliding through my house

5

In my dreams, I am able to float through the gates
You, my Lord, needed only to pass by

I have closed the shutters against the wind
Incense rises from the carved heron's beak

I remember when servant girls used to rub
Cinnabar paste on my breasts and thighs

At dawn, the eunuchs inspected us
To discover who had been unfaithful

But those are stories of better times
Tonight, I am all alone in the Palace of Clouds

Eskimo Villanelle

(for John Lees)

If this is the word, how did you know it?
Whale is good, but caribou is better.
Did you change your mind? Or did you lose it?

Can you chop ice? Have you sharpened it?
I stare at the rotting stump until supper.
If this is the place, how will I show it?

Will you mash the berries? Would you like to sit?
I never went fishing with him or his brother.
Did I change my mind? Or did I lose it?

I washed my parka and sewed the mitt.
I cannot make it go any faster.
If this is the way, I will learn to use it.

I have drawn the tree. Would you like to see it?
You must tell me the secret name of the river.
If this is the word, how will I know it?
Did you change your mind? Or did you lose it?

Eskimo Tales

He tied it with a piece of string
She covered it with a plate

Did you lose your mitt
Did you quit playing cards

She sewed it with a needle
He split it with an axe

What did you have for supper
How many fish did you catch

He fixed it with a hammer
He clubbed it with a piece of wood

Radiant Silhouette I

Blue leather harness slips off glistening shoulders
A row of whispers burns on the windowsill

The company motto: Don't count
your scalps before they're dried

I am stapled to the listening post
scanning glass beads and loose teardrops

A lean stalk of sharkskin
on a high frequency appetite surge

I am gnawing the edge of my dusty tongue
when another profile jolts the screen

slips through the twilight crevices
Camera shadow trap evaluates commodity status

defines risk probability
I remember when spring was blue and green

and ants were crushed on the museum's steps
Now, someone's emerald shadow

glows beneath the slab of a dead volcano night
and archaic language splinters

float to the surface of the dream
Do you want to watch me dance

until I evaporate
The soup is ripe

with flies
The laugh pools

have eroded
but I still miss your bee stung lips

Talk to me, the voice whispers
Talk to me, and I'm halfway home

Radiant Silhouette II

There is no place in this dark
to huddle

no music that hears us
singing

All this stood up on the world
until incendiary units filed their reports

I am the pile stranded in front of the window
monitoring her blue aluminum eyes

Someone whispers
Old habits are hard

and thin
yet she still sleeps in her hair

A woman points to herself
as if she were a foreign language

I am one of many swathed in fire
a tangerine hanging on the south wall

Bring me my head on a shoe
Bring me the remnants that are mine

so I may tend to their festering
My smile is washable

I have hurled a spear of lightning
into the camera

I have dredged it up

Radiant Silhouette III

Baudelaire took the train
from Paris to Rome

a pink skull and blue pear
balanced on the tray beside him

My mother saw hideous diseases
whenever I spoke

something to be expunged from the filthy air
he whispered

pointing to his bird wing shadow
I had to learn to erase the mirror

when I reached for the pen
ignore the ink-stained butterfly

hovering above
a painting of heaven

a popular postcard entitled *The Poet*
I once sent to my sister

I wanted to become a woman
ashamed of her breasts

their enormous size
pendulous weight

I listened to her
undressing in the dark

afraid of how she will be
described

I am a paper hat
tumbling across a desert

On a dusty windshield
someone has scribbled

xylophone
blubber breath

dumbo and bud

Radiant Silhouette IV

Frenzy softens the air.

The hardly used desire was posted on the outer panel
of the blackboard sky. Beneath rows of illustrated
fragments, someone whispers and someone listens,
and no one agrees on how many were in the bed between
one and one equals all the hours you have known or
imagined knowing another.

The inside of the walls got sticky, and tiny spots of
pink paper floated toward the rain spattered clouds.

I followed feathers down flagpoles

I stood on trains,
    sat across from
        and beside

I traced the little wigs of a tarnished button,
    and started eating the perfumed crumbs
        left out for the leper of milk

I licked peeling canisters
    until rain trickled out of
        my mouth and pockets

    I counted the insect vowels missing from the slag heap

    I inserted a strip of imitation fur into the Book of Neon

After he tied her to the bed, she handcuffed him to the stove. Dark aquamarine light slipped off the rounded edges of the upturned venetian blinds, dropping into mirrors fastened at the corners.

An old movie flickered on the outer border of their gnawed
    platform.

Radiant Silhouette V

Dear matted squirrel tongue
tendrils rise above our village

men bray at the prospect of
another coal hard dusk

children adore the bust
honoring the baby faced dictator

Dearest ape neck
why sigh in daylight

when there are kisses
you will always treat

like snakes
Fatima Fathead and Iron Josh

I lost the formula
after I followed the flagellants

to their weekly reception
and saw their treasurer

Darling hat rack
the destiny of children is postponed

I repeatedly coughed
in your rhinestone shoes

Another book of love poems
is stolen from the burning library

Dented dog dish
don't envy the esthete

in his firefly cell
Meet me behind

the Blue Hell Mambo Club
Former Lord of the Summer Purges

Fellow slime wallower
in the garden of earthly delights

Once I was as tender
as a broken wing

Bare Sheets I

We walked through the afternoon's diminishing arches until we reached evening's pink marble outskirts, and then looked for a cheap hotel. In the room, you unbuttoned your blouse and pointed to the stars swirling between your breasts. I asked about the ink drifting beneath your skin, its blue roses. That, you said, is a letter I mailed to myself one morning, shortly after emerging from the ocean.

Bare Sheets II

None of the many words we summoned to our sides fitted what we said to each other. Words and phrases, like small birds, their pulsing colors, rose up and scattered in every direction. Frantic wings tore the remaining stars further and further apart. Although winter had claimed the city, the bay windows were still open. Night or something known by that name was soaking through the last porous layers of language we had left, the ones we imagined keeping from each other. It is time to start removing our skin, you whispered, its alphabet of disguises.

Bare Sheets III

(At The Museum)
You walked past the painting, while I stopped and looked. Two lovers are kneeling beside a pond, fumbling at the margins of their reflections. You looked back and smiled. The painter has caught them in a moment of uncertainty. You went on. But are they trapped inside his fiction? Or is he trapped inside ours? I said: Yes. I said: It is not clear who is pointing to the words that are drowned each time someone speaks. Look at us, for example. The space between the words each of us whispers has started to diminish. That, you answered, started happening long before we met.

Modern Love

The clouds continued swelling like poisoned fish
While the boy listened carefully to the story
That was being invented by the girl
Who, like him, had been abandoned in the city.
They were, she whispered, itchy to avoid the forest
And reach the little red motel by the stream.

However, when she came to the edge of the stream,
She began trembling like a fish.
She was going to have to enter the forest,
After all, and hear the birds laughing at her recital of a story.
"I've become as soft and defenseless as a drug infested city.
I might as well eat rags and dust," muttered the girl.

Suddenly, the boy was scared of the girl,
And wondered how to cover the stream
Of invectives she was leaving all over their city
Owned apartment: "Perhaps, if I steal a fish.
Pick some flowers, and beg you to finish the story,
You will remember how to lead us past the forest."

Remembering that no one had ever circumnavigated the forest
Before, she tried to pretend she was just another pretty but
    deranged girl.
"Don't be afraid: If you happen to fall off the edge of my story,
Remember that paper is made from trees that have crashed into a
    stream.
It is only frightening if you are a fish."
She put on her best stupid smile and she looked out at the city

Which had spread further than any other city.
Still, no one had been able to map the forest.
"Before you go out and cadge a fish,
I should teach you how to swim," said the girl.
"There is something lurking at the bottom of the stream,
And it may attempt to break into my story."

This happens every time she tells a story,
He thought, as evening's shadows absorbed the city.
I can no longer be sure of the meaning of "stream."
Or what is immeasurable about the forest.
If I am lucky, I will be able to convince the next girl
That life's pleasures consist of warm rows of oily fish.

"Actually, the story is about two fish
Who leave their stream to live in the forest.
It is a parable about our life in the city,"
                              began the girl.

Printed September 1989 in Santa Barbara & Ann Arbor for the Black Sparrow Press by Graham Mackintosh & Edwards Brothers Inc. Design by Barbara Martin. This edition is published in paper wrappers; there are 250 hardcover trade copies; 125 hardcover copies have been numbered & signed by the author; & 26 numbered copies handbound in boards by Earle Gray are lettered & signed by the author.

Photo: Editha Mesina

JOHN YAU was born in Lynn, Massachusetts on June 5, 1950. He studied at Bard College (B.A., 1972) and Brooklyn College (M.F.A., 1977). Since 1978, he has written for such magazines as *Art in America, Artforum, Art News, Flash Art,* and *Vogue,* contributed essays to monographs, curated exhibitions, and taught at Bard College (Milton Avery Graduate School of the Arts), Brooklyn College, Emerson College, and Maryland Institute College of Art. He is a Contributing Editor to *ARTS Magazine, Contemporanea, Cover,* and *Sulfur,* and teaches in the Graduate Program at Pratt Institute and the School of Visual Arts.

His publications include *Crossing Canal Street, Sometimes, Broken Off by the Music,* and *Corpse and Mirror,* which was chosen by John Ashbery to appear in the National Poetry Series. He has received Fellowships from the National Endowment for the Arts and the Ingram Merrill Foundation. In 1988, he received a fellowship from the New York Foundation of the Arts, a General Electric Foundation Award, and the Lavan Award from the Academy of American Poets. Since the mid 1980s, he has collaborated with a number of contemporary artists on book, print, and mixed media projects. He lives and works in Manhattan.